To our Ro

thanks for your iiii(p)
Goff.

A BOWL OF SCOUSE

John Patrick Kerrigan

Other releases by John Patrick Kerrigan:
Liverpool The Gateway to America

Multimedia DVDs:
Liverpool The Gateway to America
North Liverpool Now and Then
Liverpool American Links

First Published 2009 by Countyvise Limited,
14 Appin Road, Birkenhead, Wirral CH41 9HH.

British Library Cataloguing in Publication Data.
A catalogue record for this book is available from the British Library.

ISBN 978 1 906823 21 4

ACKNOWLEDGEMENTS

Except for general historical information, the primary facts in this publication were researched personally from public and private institutions, online from Internet sources, The Liverpool Record Office, and from a number of individuals and resource centres.

I would also like to acknowledge my parents, Pat and Peggy Kerrigan for their consideration and considerable foresight, in ensuring that I would be born as a citizen of this great city of Liverpool. Thanks guys.

To my wife Barbara, daughters Julie and Laura, grandchildren - Ben, Ciara, Alex, and Anya, thanks for all your support over the last two years.

INTRODUCTION

Starters: This book could have been given a grand title such as 'A Potpourri Of Liverpool History', or perhaps 'An Eclectic History of Liverpool', but a more practical and less pretentious title was required, something with a uniquely Liverpool flavour, how about a - *A Bowl of Scouse*?

This book will cover a selection of significant, but perhaps lesser known events - stories of people and places from Liverpool's incredibly varied history.

It tells of various locations around Liverpool as they are today, and recalls some of the fascinating events which have taken place there in the past, but are now almost forgotten.

For instance, there are at least two different locations in the North Liverpool area, which link to the disastrous loss of the Titanic.

The tragic family story of Henry Tingle Wilde, Chief Officer of the Titanic, and his family, who was born in Highfield Road, Walton and lived with his family in Grey Road, off Rice Lane.

The fascinating story of the 'Two Gold Watches', concerning Titanic crew member Thomas Hewitt who lived with his wife Ada and family in Devonfield Road, Orrell Park. A romantic, but ultimately tragic story.

Another highly dramatic, but little known event from the First World War concerns the Court Martial held at Grace Road Barracks, in Liverpool, of Canadian soldiers who had taken part in a mutiny at Kinmel Camp, St Asaph in North Wales in 1919.

The author Robert Tressell who wrote a famous book about English working class life in the early 1900s - and died in a Liverpool Workhouse, was eventually found to be buried in a pauper grave in Rice Lane Cemetery.

Other equally fascinating stories featured in this book include -

- The survivor who was buried under tons of rubble in the bombing of the Windsor Castle Pub in 1941 during the May Blitz.
- The infamous murder at The Old Curiosity Shop in Warbreck Moor Aintree,
- The role of the Aintree Racecourse, in both the First and Second World Wars.
- The good old days at the Aintree Institute, when it was a whole 20p to see The Beatles play live.
- Why were British Army Cavalry needed to escort prison vans to Walton Gaol in 1911?
- A nostalgic look at the cinemas and picture houses which seemed to be on every other street corner.
- The truth behind the legend of Adolf Hitler's supposed visit to south Liverpool in 1911.
- The tragic circumstances which brought about the

foundation of the NSPCC in 19th century Liverpool.

- The things we never had then, and might perhaps take for granted today.
- The day the American President's wife came to Liverpool.

These fascinating stories and the answers to many more questions, relating to long forgotten incidents from  Liverpool's past, can be found here. It's to be hoped that the contents of the book, like the ingredients of a Bowl of Scouse, will be warm and nourishing, simple, enjoyable, and easily digested - but above all, will have some of the unmistakable taste of Liverpool.

Scouse was originally brought to Liverpool by Scandinavian sailors, and called 'Labskause'.

This was eventually shortened to Skause and over time the spelling changed to the version we use today, Scouse. The people who ate Scouse were generally sailors and their families and eventually all sailors from Liverpool were referred to as Scousers.

Today, those who are from the region of Liverpool are usually known as Scousers. Scouse is somewhere between Lancashire Hotpot and Irish Stew, just as Liverpool is situated somewhere between Ireland and Lancashire, and the dish continues to hold a place in the heart of Liverpudlian's as the taste of their hometown, and today, is regularly eaten by a great number of families in the area.

Recipe for a Bowl of Scouse -

Serves 4-6 people (or one Mancunian).
Half a Pound of Stewing Steak, Half a Pound of Lamb's Breast, A Large Onion. 1lb of Carrots, 5lb of Potatoes, 2 Oxo Cubes, 2 Teaspoons of Vegetable Oil, Salt and Pepper, Water

HOW TO COOK
Cut the meat into large cubes and fry in the vegetable oil until lightly browned all over. You may wish to add some Worcester Sauce at this point for added flavour. Transfer the meat to a large saucepan and add the chopped onion.

Follow this by chopping the carrot into slices and place this on the meat.

Peel and then finely dice 1lb of the potatoes and place on top of the carrots.Fill the pan with cold water until it is half full. Break up the Oxo cubes and sprinkle into the water.

Add salt and pepper for seasoning. Let the pan simmer gently, stirring occasionally. The large pieces of onion will start to break up and the potato will become soft and make the final sauce thicker. Simmer for a total of two hours, then add the remaining potatoes. These are peeled and roughly chopped, along with a few splashes of HP Brown Sauce. Then simmer for another two hours and serve piping hot with red cabbage, and crusty bread.

Blind Scouse was a variation on the above recipe and mostly eaten by poorer people, as it was cheaper to make, and it did not contain any meat. (You may even call it Vegetarian Scouse - if you wanted to sound a bit posh). The dish was served as a treat to those lucky people in the workhouses of 19th century Lancashire.

Try this out at your next dinner party - Invite your friends and neighbours to come with scouse wigs on and dressed in 'hoodies' and 'trackie bottoms'.

Then give each of them a bowl of scouse and a pint of 'brown mixed'.

Now they will quite easily be able to say things like -

"Gerra blimp of dis boss scouse 'ere , yer wanna get sum of dis scran down ya - its sound mate". Translation - Look at this superb casserole we have here, you really have to try some of this food, it's excellent my friend.

After reading this book, I hope you will agree that there is a lot more to Liverpool than just 'Harry Enfield's Scousers', although they can still be found here and there. There is a place for everyone in Liverpool.

MENU

CHAPTER ONE

A Beatles Institution

The Aintree Institute was built by local industrialist Sir William Hartley [1846-1922] in 1890 as a social hall for the workers from his famous Jam Factory at Long Lane.

He also built, about the same time, the Methodist Chapel at Cedar Road 500 yards away.

In a biographical account of his life, it described him as:

"Very desirous of co-operation in humanitarian work between all the Churches." This was never more clearly expressed by him than in connection with the movement for establishing an Institute in Aintree. The suggestion came from him, and so he offered £1,000 towards the project.

At a meeting on March 4, 1892, he opened the discussion, and said that the reform he would like to see in the district was that all the Churches, from the Roman Catholic Church and the Church of England to the very smallest mission room, should enter into a compact to fight evil in every form.

He hoped that in the near future the combined Churches in that neighbourhood would erect in some central position a large building, containing a concert and lecture hall and, if possible, a gymnasium and reading room. The chief underlying idea that struck him as new was that the work should be run by a committee of all the Churches. It would then be known as the rendezvous of all good works, where all, no matter what their religious creed, might meet to promote all good objects.

The cost would depend on the amount of money they could raise; anything from £3,000 to £10,000 might be spent on the building.

The work would be carried on at a low cost if it was carried on in the vigorous and Christ like manner he would like to see, and he was quite prepared to subscribe £50 a year towards this cost.

If the scheme was approved, he suggested that a Committee should be formed of half a dozen persons from each Church, including the minister, and that it should have a free hand in determining cost, style and accommodation.

The suggestion did not prove acceptable. More than two and a half years later he spoke again upon the subject.

He said how he desired in this district, a centre and rallying point for everything that was elevating and of a Christian character.

He would endeavour to bring into line every person in the community for humanitarian works - everyone who desired to serve his fellows. He had done his best during the past two years or more to arouse some local sympathy in such a practical form so as to result in the erection of a suitable premises. His efforts, unfortunately, had been unsuccessful. He did not feel that he was called upon to provide such a centre, but he saw no chance of it being provided in any other way, he therefore had decided to do the work himself, entirely on his own responsibility.

His plan was to give a site of nearly three acres which would be laid out as a recreation ground with bowling greens and tennis grounds, a cafe was to be built with two billiard rooms and private dining rooms, and with a work men's restaurant, specially designed for the carters who in large numbers daily passed along the two roads on which the cafe stood.

A large space was provided where the horses could be fed, and the scheme also included large stables. A hall, to accommodate 650 people, measuring 64 by 40 feet, with balconies, was part of the plan.

This would be fitted up with a stage and the roof constructed in such a way that when the hall was not otherwise in use, it could be used as a gymnasium. Class-rooms and a lecture-room would complete the building on the educational side.

The Institute and Cafe, costing with subsequent extensions £12,000, was thus provided entirely by Mr Hartley in 1896. It was opened by the Earl of Derby, who was at the time Lord Mayor of Liverpool, Mr Hartley himself being then a member of the Liverpool City Council. *"It has also served a very useful purpose for indoor and outdoor recreation and also for education, and it has proved of value in its provision of refreshment free, from the temptations of the public-house".*

All that remains of Hartley's Factory, 2005

Mr Hartley was one of the first to provide a dining-room for his workers with the men and women having separate accommodation. The dining-hall for the women, measures 82 feet by 42 feet. The men's dining-room is naturally much smaller; it measures 36 feet by 17 feet. In these rooms 750 can dine at once. They are on the ground floor together with the stores, pantries, etc. The provision for cooking, which includes a large bakery, is on a very elaborate scale since, in the height of the season, 1,000 to 1,500 dinners have to be prepared every day.

As the rooms are in use for several hours in the day and during this time 3,000 to 4,000 meals are served, the question of ventilation is of great importance.

Immense trouble had been taken to secure the best system, and Mr Hartley, in company with the architect, visited a considerable number of buildings, so as to secure not only the best general system but to avoid regrettable mistakes in detail. The atmosphere can be renewed, and it is purified

Hartley's Factory viewed from Long Lane, 1927

before it is forced into the rooms and warmed in cold weather to whatever temperature is required. It was his desire that everything in the cooking department should be both nice and cheap. Accordingly, all arrangements were made that the food should be as well prepared and as cheap as possible.

Close to the works Mr Hartley also erected a model village. Rental including rates, taxes and water was from two shillings 6d. a week. A number of five-roomed cottages were available to let for three shillings. 6d. a week. He also built several better houses to be sold at cost price to working men, including others, as well as his own workpeople.

His method was to charge 3¾ per cent on the amount of the purchase money and for part of the principal to be paid off each month, the repayment being completed within a period of 20 years.

As far back as his early Aintree period Mr Hartley was keenly interested in the question of housing which by now had become acute.

The cottages for the workpeople were provided with

gardens, the streets were wide, there was a central bowling green and a field for football and hockey. It must be considered as quite an enlightened, if paternal, view of employer and workforce relationship for its time.

Alongside the Institute main hall, an additional mock Tudor building had been constructed to provide a canteen for Hartley's employees.

It was adapted into a cafe in the 1950s and became known as 'The Bermuda Cafe'. During World War Two, the Institute was used as a dance hall for American servicemen who were based at Aintree racecourse.

The building was later purchased by the local Catholic church as a social club for its parishioners during the 1950s. In the early 1960s the concert hall became a premier venue for the beat groups which were springing up all over Liverpool at that time.

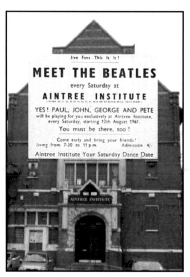

THE BEATLES

The Aintree Institute was one of many local Dance Halls that were seen as a 'step up' from playing the usual bars and cellar clubs of Liverpool. Even though The Beatles had played regularly at the "Sensational Jive Dances" held at the Institute since January, it was not until 12 August 1961 that promoter

Brian Kelly hired "The Dynamic Beatles" as Saturday night regulars. The gig lasted for seven weeks. Brian Kelly, a great supporter of the group since May 1960, booked the band for nearly 60 appearances at the Institute and also at Litherland Town Hall in 1961 alone.

They performed over 31 times at the Aintree Institute, which had featured live music and community events until it was demolished recently.

The Institute was described at the time as being 'frequented by rough patrons who have a habit of tossing chairs at other people, including the group on stage'.

Hard though it may be to imagine, most of those who were formerly patrons of the Aintree Institute in 1961, would by now be eligible to attend one of the senior citizens lunch clubs in the Institute.

Sadly, due to yet another act of cultural vandalism, the Aintree

Calling all Jive Fans !

HAVE YOU HEARD ABOUT THE

SENSATIONAL

JIVE DANCES

every

FRIDAY & SATURDAY

7-45 to 11 p.m.   7-30 to 11 p.m.

3/-   4/-

at AINTREE INSTITUTE

BUSES TO DOOR

20 20e 22 35 61 91 92 92a 93 95 96 500

every Saturday features

THE DYNAMIC BEATLES

★ TELL YOUR FRIENDS THE GREAT NEWS ★

COME ONE   COME ALL

TO AINTREE INSTITUTE !

for the best in jive on Friday and Saturday nights

BEEKAY PROMOTIONS.

Institute is no more - demolished to make way for the site of yet another shopping complex.

Maybe the ghostly sound of the Beatles music, suspended in the ether, may bring back distant memories to some of those former 'Jive Fans' as they pass the demolition site which has now replaced the former Aintree Institute.

Nowadays they are probably on their way to the Post Office at the Black Bull, to collect their old age pensions.

The Aintree Institute was the original home of the Aintree Action for Justice & Peace Group which celebrated 45 years of Justice & Peace Working in the community.

Easter 2008 marked the 45th anniversary of the Aintree Action Group - who went on to become the founders of the longest serving Justice & Peace group in the UK. It was partially inspired by the cultural changes during the early 1960s, and from the awesome struggles of the American Civil Rights movement and the courageous leadership of Rev Dr Martin Luther King Jr - and even though much water has passed under the bridge since that time, the original principles of seeking justice and peace for those in need - both locally and globally, are still very much their guiding principles.

It all began in March of 1963 when a group of friends living in North Liverpool were discussing their concerns about the plight of some elderly members of the community, many of whom had been severely affected by the unusually harsh winter. They realised that they could utilise basic skills in plumbing and redecorating, skills which we already had in our own community, to help those old people living in rented houses.

Many elderly people in the area, who owned their own homes, but were without the means to seek professional help, had been badly hit when the deep frost had frozen the old lead water pipes over the previous few months, had begun to burst the water pipes now that they were thawing so flooding out their houses, and for whom no provision for helping them was available at that time.

And so they began to organise repairs and to re-decorate the badly damaged properties from within the resources of their own community.

At this time, they also decided to try to help the Freedom from Hunger Campaign, which was at that time raising awareness and funds for the hungry in the third world. During the last 45 years, the Aintree Action and Overseas Aid Group has developed, and continues to develop those principles, with some of the original members still active today.

The Group became a Registered Charity about 30 years ago and moved more into fund-raising in order to answer the many calls for help it received.

They opened a shop called Small Change in Orrell Park in 1980 and have continued to operate the shop using volunteers. This community charity has raised a substantial sum each year since, which has been used for the benefit of homeless people in Liverpool, and to support a large number of projects in the developing world.

One of the first night shelters for the homeless in Liverpool was started by John Jennings, called the Simon Community. It was started with funding and support from the group and continues to operate under a different name to this day.

Currently they are helping to support homeless men and women at a unit run by the Sisters of Mother Theresa in Liverpool. The Group were privileged to meet Mother Theresa on two of the occasions when she visited Liverpool, to discuss working to help the homeless. They are still fully committed to helping this unit for the homeless on a regular monthly basis.

From the beginning it was accepted that the enormous problems of disease and starvation facing people in the so called 'third world' would still be with us for the foreseeable future, and so, much of their fund raising has been directed to a variety of small self-help schemes in the developing world, mainly involving the growing of food, and hygiene, sanitation, women's empowerment, education and general improvements to the quality of life. These problems remain a major problem, now, and in the future. Since those early days of campaigning for change, there have in fact been many changes, sadly these have not always been changes for the better.

"We think sometimes that poverty is only being hungry, naked and homeless. The poverty of being unwanted, unloved and uncared for, that is the greatest poverty".
Mother Teresa - On Poverty

'There are places I remember all my life,
Though some have changed,
Some forever, not for better
Some have gone and some remain.
All these places have their moments
Some are dead and some are living
In my life, I loved them all
I know I'll never lose affection for
people and things that went before
And I know I'll often stop and think about them'.

'In My Life'   ©Lennon & McCartney.

CHAPTER TWO

More than just a Racecourse

Internationally known, Aintree Racecourse has long been famous as the home of the Grand National Steeplechase.

The first official races at Aintree were organised by a syndicate, headed by the owner of Liverpool's Waterloo Hotel, Mr William Lynn.

He leased the land from Lord Sefton, set out a course and built a grandstand. Lord Molyneux laid the foundation stone on February 7, 1829 and placed a bottle full of sovereigns in the footings.

The course staged its initial jump fixture in 1835. On Tuesday, February 26, 1839, Lottery became the first winner of the Grand National. In those days the horses had to jump a stone wall, cross a stretch of ploughed land and finish over two hurdles.

The race was then known as the Grand Liverpool Steeplechase.

Mr Lynn was responsible for turning the National into a handicap in 1843 after it had been a weight-for-age race for the first four years. A Mr Topham took over the lease of Aintree in 1848 and became Clerk of the Course. The Topham family owned substantial tracts of land around Aintree and in 1949 they bought the course outright from Lord Sefton. Aintree suffered lean times in the post-war years. In 1965, it was announced that the course would be sold to a property developer. This started one of the longest periods of uncertainty in the history of British sport, with endless speculation about the future.

Red Rum the racehorse achieved an unmatched historic treble when he won the Grand National in 1973, 1974 and 1977. He came second in 1975 and 1976 and in his first two victories, he was ridden by Brian Fletcher. The following year Stack rode him to his triumphant third Grand National, considered one of the greatest moments in British sporting history.

Not surprisingly, Red Rum became one of the best known and most loved of racehorses.

The 2005 National saw the start of another significant era in the Liverpool course's history. John Smith's, a subsidiary of Scottish & Newcastle, sponsored the Grand National and many of the other races at the three-day meeting for the first time.

The impact of John Smith's sponsorship was immediately felt and will continue until 2010, after an early extension of the contract.

A fictional account of a young girl training the winner of the Grand National at Aintree, from a book by Enid Bagnold, was made into a film called National Velvet. It starred the young Elizabeth Taylor as the heroine, Velvet Brown. The American made film was quite a big box office hit at the time.

Another film based on the events surrounding the 1981 National and the winning jockey, Bob Champion, were also dramatised in the film 'Champions'.

The motor-racing circuit, which still circles the Grand National track, was constructed in 1954 and was another of Mrs Topham's innovations. It hosted a European Grand Prix and five British Grand Prix.

The car racing track was first used in 1954, was three miles in length and very fast, and as a result it quickly rose to prominence in the austerity of post-war Britain, with Aintree being picked to host the British Grand Prix in 1955. Currently the Aintree car circuit plays

host to the Aintree Motorcycle Racing Club, which stages various motorcycle racing events throughout the year.

Twenty First Century Aintree The new Aintree International Equestrian Centre - completed in 2007, was designed specifically to provide a venue for Equestrianism, and is now a showpiece in itself.

Aintree International Equestrian Centre also boasts some of the very best facilities for equine stars of the future. The versatile arena is not only a centre of excellence for equestrian pursuits, it also provides the perfect setting for large exhibitions, conferences and corporate dinners.

The Racecourse during the first World War

Racecourse Retail Park

Today, alongside the Aintree Racecourse is the Aintree Retail Park.

The site of the Retail Park has previously been home in the past, to an aircraft factory, a World War One armament factory, and in World War Two, a French Navy camp and later during WW2, a huge US Army camp. The original large factory complex at Aintree was built in the First World

War by the British government, to manufacture aircraft, and then in a separate group of buildings on the site there was a shell manufacturing facility. Three national aircraft factories were established by the Cunard Steamship Co in 1917 and started production the following year.

Women at work inside National Aircraft Factory No. 3 in 1917

The Aintree factory's objective was to aid the war effort by building 500 Bristol Fighters to supply the new and rapidly-growing Royal Air Force.

Production was under the auspices of the newly-created Air Ministry and 126 aircraft had been built by the time the war ended in November 1918.

The chairman of Cunard, at that time, Sir Alfred Booth, told *The New York Times* in June 1919:

"We were associated from the start with the immense aeroplane factory at Aintree. The foundations were begun in October 1917 and the first aeroplanes were turned out in June 1918, eight months later."

He also reported to The New York Times that, *"the branch engine shop in Rimrose Road Bootle was converted late in 1915 into a shell factory employing 1000 people of whom about 90%, were women.*

The total output of the factory, until it was closed down in 1918 after the Armistice, amounted to 450,000 shells.

It was a cause of great satisfaction to Cunard Ltd that we were able to help the country, to some slight extent, in a great emergency."

It must have given even greater satisfaction to the Cunard shareholders when Sir Alfred disclosed that the assets of the company had increased from £6.6 million to £15 million.

Cunard also owned a site at Rimrose Road in Bootle, where they had a munitions factory making bombs and shells. This image shows women at work making shell cases in the Cunard armaments factory at Rimrose Road Bootle, for use during World War I (1914-1918).

During the 1930s a Dutch company, *Eerste Nederlandse Kunstzijdefabriek Arnhem*, based at Arnhem in Holland, re-opened the former ammunition factory as a rayon artificial textile facility, to be known as the British Enka Artificial Silk Co Ltd, where among other things they made artificial silk for parachutes during the second world war.

It was eventually acquired after the war by Courtaulds Ltd, and they continued to manufacture synthetic fibres at

Enka Spinning Room

Aintree until its closure during the 1970s. The UK recession and the increase in international competition placed severe pressure on Courtauld's textiles and clothing businesses. A major rationalisation process led to withdrawal from a number of commodity product businesses which were unable to compete internationally on price, and closures soon followed at a large number of its plants throughout Britain, including Aintree.

The Racecourse during the Second World War

During the early part of the Second World War the racecourse site became part of the allied war effort, initially as a camp for French Navy personnel after the fall of France to the Nazis.

Later, in 1943, the site was used as a base for thousands of US Army soldiers and airmen, in preparation for D-Day.

Liverpool is fondly remembered by U.S. servicemen who were stationed at the many bases in and around the city, such as Aintree, Maghull, and Haydock.

A former US Serviceman, Mr Ralph Boyd from Illinois, was based in wartime Liverpool, and wrote in a letter to the author:

"We landed in Glasgow, Scotland, on December 15, 1942, and was then taken to Liverpool by train.

They would bus us each day from Kirkby to Liverpool so we could work on the docks with the 15th Port Mobil T.C. (Transportation Corps).

Our job at Liverpool was to supervise the unloading and the shipping of supplies to other depots for the troops on the line.

We worked about 27 miles of dock at Liverpool and also across the river at Birkenhead. The average age of the people working on the docks was 45 to 60 since most of the young men were in service.

They were very good people to work with, and very hard workers.

Sometimes we worked as many as six to seven ships at a time. This kept you pretty busy, riding the overhead from one dock to the other.

We sometimes had to depend on the civilians to keep track of the material shipped because we were so busy.

In September 1999, we went to the England with my Sister-in-law and her husband to visit their son and his family. They took us to Liverpool.

At the Pier Head we saw the acknowledgement to the people of Liverpool, thanking them for their help to the 15th Port Unit - US Army."

The following is an extract from an article written by the author for the BBC Web site titled 'WW2 - The Peoples War'.

'It was 1943 and I was then five years old, when suddenly, everything seemed to change in Liverpool.

The American Army had arrived and overnight everything seemed to change from black and white to colour.

I was reminded of this event, which happened over 60 years ago, when visiting my daughter and her family in Utah, USA some years ago.

I was in a small town called Ogden in Utah , visiting the local railway museum, and talking to one of the guides there who mentioned that the Union Pacific Station had been at the crossroads of the many wartime military training camps in the area. It was from here that many US soldiers would set out on the first leg of their long journey to Britain and begin their preparations for the invasion of Europe on D Day.

It prompted me to think about my own memories of those times, when as a small boy, I watched with fascination, as a succession of troop ships after arriving at Liverpool's Pierhead Landing Stage, began their six mile march to the new camp that had been established at Aintree Racecouse.

I can still clearly remember the thousands of GI's marching in columns along Walton Vale, as I came out of school.

They were followed by enormous trucks, jeeps, tankers and every conceivable type of military vehicle.

They were marching from the docks to take up residence at the world famous Aintree Racecourse — the home of the Grand National.

Eventually over 1600 of them were camped there, with the racecourse turned into a vast parking lot for military vehicles and equipment.

Distant memories of individuals like the GI who was walking towards my sister and I as we walked home from school along Moss Lane. He was carrying a large box of chocolates tied up with a ribbon. He asked if we liked Candy — 'What is it?' we said, but then quickly added, 'Yes please'. He had obviously failed to impress one of the local girls, but he certainly impressed us.

And of the time when a trio of musicians in uniform came into our classroom at school and mercifully relieved us from our boredom by playing some swing music. Or how they never seemed to tire of being asked countless times 'Got any gum chum' by hordes of local kids.

The Americans soon took over cafes, milk bars, and pubs and dance halls. One of them, the Aintree Institute, later became better known as one of the venues of The Beatles in the sixties A stone plaque was erected at the Pier Head Liverpool to commemorate the fact that over a million US soldiers passed through the port on their way to take part in D day. Many would later return in one of the thousands of military coffins stored in a vast warehouse on the waterfront.

But that was a part of the war I was yet to discover.

After the heavy bombing which had already devastated large parts of the city during the May Blitz of 1941, the war

HERE IN THE DARK DAYS OF WAR

AND IN THE DAWN OF VICTORY

AMERICAN TROOPS AND CARGOES

MOVED THROUGH THIS PORT

FURTHERED BY BRITISH AND AMERICANS

WORKING TOGETHER

THIS STONE RECORDS THEIR UNITY

IN ACCOMPLISHING THEIR MISSION

ERECTED BY THE 15th PORT UNIT

UNITED STATES ARMY. 1944

had now became an exhilarating and colourful experience for us small boys, with the continuing excitement of so many new people and events happening almost daily all around us.

At the end of the war, the American forces departed as quickly as they had arrived, and the Racecourse slowly returned to normal, leaving hardly a trace behind.

It now appears that despite all the pain and suffering that brought about the eventual victory over the enemy that what lasts in the end is the bonds of our common humanity. Now whenever I pass the racecourse at Aintree, I recall those times 60 years ago when Little America came to visit us in 1943 and then quietly went back home in 1944, and of the many little acts of kindness which these strange and colourful allies brought to our community during those dark and dangerous times. '

Aintree Racecourse soon become a gigantic vehicle park to

store the huge quantity of vehicles and equipment arriving at Liverpool Docks, where vital war supplies and equipment arrived aboard merchant ships sailing from America, and carried to Liverpool in huge convoys across the Atlantic.

Liverpool was Britain's most important port during the second world war. It handled one third of the country's war imports and was the main terminal for Atlantic convoys. By early 1941, it had also become headquarters of Britain's North Atlantic campaign. An average of four convoys of cargo ships a week arrived from the USA in the Mersey during the war and between 1939 and 1945 the Port of Liverpool handled over 75 million tons of cargo. In addition almost 74,000 aeroplanes and gliders were brought into the port, with well over 4.7 million troops passing through Liverpool - en route to Normandy, of whom 1.2 million were American. In November 1942, Mrs Eleanor Roosevelt made a secret visit to Liverpool as part of her UK tour to help boost the morale of US troops based here, and in addition, to try to help bolster wartime Anglo-American relations. The President's wife had been a supporter of the early civil rights movement in pre-war America and was opposed to the official policy of racial segregation which existed, and was firmly established in the military at that time - and which was to continue for another 30 years.

The image shown overleaf shows Mrs Roosevelt, inspecting troops at the segregated US Army camp in Deyes Lane at Maghull in 1942.

The Maghull Camp was for black soldiers and white officers, and was run in conjunction with the camp at

Afro-American Troops Maghull. 1944

Aintree Racecourse which was exclusively for white US service men, with an officers mess and billet at what is now the Admin Buildings at the Kirkby Industrial Estate.

Then just as suddenly as they had arrived, the American forces were gone, leaving very little evidence that they had ever been here. There was however a human legacy which remained afterwards, in the form of children who sadly never got to know their fathers.

There are tens of thousands of children fathered by American GIs during the war in countries such as England, France, Netherlands and post war in Germany and Austria, the forgotten children of World War II. Most of these children grew up fatherless - in many cases their American fathers either died in the war or returned home not aware of the existence of their child. Over the years, there was little or no notice taken in the mainstream press of the existence of these now aging children, some of whom still continue to search for a link to their biological families. It is estimated by US government sources that during World War Two, in excess of 183,000 children were left fatherless by American servicemen on foreign soil.

CHAPTER THREE

Three Remarkable Ladies

Apparently there is a biblical quotation which says 'no one is a prophet in their own land' - in other words, some of the greatest members of our Liverpool family, are not necessarily those whom we immediately recognise as such. In this chapter I will tell about three ladies born here in Liverpool, two of them have become legends in the third world countries in which they have spent their lives with the poorest of the poor, but hardly noticed here in their hometown - incidentally, nor would they expect to be.

Dr Anne Merriman

Dr. Anne Merriman grew up in the West Derby area of Liverpool. Even at the early age of four, Anne had an interest in working overseas, declaring to her mother that when she grew up she would like to go and work in Africa. She fulfilled her early wishes a year after graduating from medical school in Dublin, when she became medical officer at a busy hospital in Nigeria. However it was back in her birthplace of Liverpool, working as a consultant and senior lecturer in geriatric medicine during the '70s, that Anne first developed an interest in palliative care.

She stated that she became acutely aware of the need for special care in many 'end of life situations', and particularly an improvement to their quality of life, and assisting the terminally ill to end their lives in peace.

After completing a masters degree in international community health in 1982, Anne spent time in Malaysia and then in Singapore.

While researching palliative care needs, she soon felt drawn to try to meet the terrible needs she had unearthed.

She later helped to set up a volunteer group, now the Hospice Care Association which cares for 60% of patients with cancer in Singapore.

The charity support group Hospice Africa is based here on Merseyside, and was set up by friends and former colleagues of Dr Anne's as a UK registered charity, and founded in August 1993. It is committed to providing, or supporting the provision of palliative care to cancer and HIV/AIDS patients in Sub-Saharan Africa, but draws its supporters from all over the UK and indeed world-wide.

It operates principally as a fund-raising organisation, but also provides advice and support to its partners in sub-Saharan Africa. The work of the charity is carried out entirely by a dedicated team of volunteers and nobody receives a salary. Their aim is to ensure that administrative costs are kept to a minimum and ensure that as much money as possible reaches those who need it in Africa.

Dr. Merriman has edited several publications and has published extensively; she has also received numerous international awards in recognition of her hard work and success in improving the care of patients in Africa and Asia.

Dr Anne summed up her remarkable achievements and life's work quite simply - "I am from Liverpool and we can smile about many things, because of the fun to be found in life."

Dora Scarlett

Dora Scarlett, 1905 - 2001, was noted as a writer, broadcaster, communist activist, and above all as the founder and driving force of an organisation providing medical care to the poor in India. The daughter of a Liverpool schoolteacher, Dora grew up in quite modest surroundings in the south end of the city. She had very strong memories of her Liverpool childhood, of the docks, and the strange plants in the Sefton park glasshouse. Dora always retained a slight Liverpool accent even though she spent most of her adult life overseas. With her intelligence and flair for writing she shone at school, but refused the expected move to university. She was more interested in horticulture, she told her parents.

She became involved with the Communist party, and after the war went at the party's instruction to Hungary to work as a broadcaster for Radio Budapest. She was supposed to beam stories of communist paradise to a British audience but found herself increasingly disillusioned with communism - and equally taken with the peasant life of eastern Europe. When the Soviet invasion came in 1956 Dora left in a hurry, with the help of the British Embassy.

Back in London, she left the party and wrote a book about her experiences called *Window Onto Hungary*.

She spent several less than happy years in London, stifled by urban life and dead end jobs. In 1959, without telling a soul, she left Britain. Six weeks later she was in Madras, having travelled by cargo ship. Dora was soon working in a village clinic outside Madras and had found again that lifelong love - the simple rural life.

After two years she felt ready to commit herself to India. She had formed a friendship with a local farmer and his wife, and together they went deep into south India, finally settling some way west of the ancient temple city of Madurai, in the foothills of the Western Ghats that run down the spine of India. Here was a place remote from the modern world, with empty land and little in the way of medical facilities. Dora sometimes recalled those early days - of what must have been the high spot of her life. Of finding the land, divining water, digging an open well, the first crops on hitherto unused soil. She told of trudging from village to village with a bag of basic medicines, learning how people lived. And she had special memories of the first western volunteers - American Peace Corps at the time of Vietnam - and how they toiled all day in the heat digging pits to plant the coconut trees that now ring the place she called Seva Nilayam, or Home of Service.

Everything was to be modest - the buildings of mud and tile in the local style, no vehicles, traditional farming methods, certainly antibiotics where needed, but simple homespun medicine where they weren't. Seva Nilayam soon had a reputation for caring as well as effective treatment and for being welcoming to the poorest and least regarded. For Dora the poor were always the focus and the reason for giving free treatment - without which the poor would never attend Seva Nilayam attracted interest around the world.

Volunteers came from the US, Australia, Sweden and Britain and funding from Switzerland, Denmark, Australia, the US and Britain. The centre took in "in patients" , but not conventionally on rows of beds in wards. Rather, these were patients who needed rest and good food as much as treatment, or who lived too far away to attend daily.

Seva Nilyam - Women at Work

The in-patients were part of the community, some staying a few days or weeks, others much longer so that they became part of the place. They helped out in the farm, garden, kitchen or clinic, in an environment not much different from their village. In the 1970s a new challenge arose. Western development agencies were moving to more progressive policies - preferring preventive to curative medical work. Dora's philosophy was that westerners had no right to impose their views on what Indian society might or might not need. She was there to provide what was asked of her, if she could. Undeterred by the loss of funding from agencies, she became her own fundraiser.

Sitting on a wooden stool in a mud walled building bashing at a 1920s typewriter, she composed a letter that started: '*I am writing to you from a remote corner of India*', and mailed copies to all the people she could think of. Dora's style was far removed from modern assertive fundraising techniques. She believed if you simply stated your need, people would respond. And they did. Soon Dora was writing a twice monthly newsletter; not appealing for money but describing the life she saw around her in clinic, village or further afield in India, and adding her insight to what she thought it all amounted to. Many compared her beliefs to those of Gandhi - whom she had met in the 1930s when he visited London. She recalled taking early morning walks with him in the East End and being deeply impressed by his presence.

But she always insisted her ideas were her own, worked out herself, not taken from others. Dora remained active in the clinic and writing to well beyond the age that many retire.

But as disabilities of sight and hearing grew in old age she stepped back and the Seva Nilayam board appointed a director to manage the organisation.

She remained at Seva Nilayam, taking an interest in the clinic and garden, and in turn being cared for, as she coped with increasing disability.

Throughout her life, her real love was gardening, and living a simple rural existence. From very simple beginnings it grew and today it includes three health and development organisations working with hundreds of thousands of poor and marginalised people.

In her later years Dora returned to practising the Catholicism of her upbringing. But Seva Nilayam had always embraced all faiths, indeed it was predominantly Hindu in its customs, so when she died, naturally Dora's funeral followed local custom.

Hundreds of local people attended the simple burial service in the beautiful garden she had created at Seva Nilayam.

This exceptional woman was made an MBE in 1994.

Bessie Braddock. My earliest recollection of Bessie Braddock takes me back to 1943 and attending a hearing of

the Public Assistance Board with my family in Liverpool.

My recently widowed mother with two children aged six and seven had to appear before the Public Assistance Board to appeal against the refusal of her application for an increase in allowance, after the death of my father.

The National Assistance Act 1948 and National Health Service Act 1946 came into effect from 5 July 1948 and brought the end of the Poor Law. Public Assistance Committees ceased to exist and their functions were transferred to various Government Departments.

Three members sat on the bench, one of which was Mrs Elizabeth Braddock MP. They had to consider whether a disputed individual claim would be granted.

I don't know what the outcome was, I guess it was negative, I do know that my mother always recalled how Bessie had put her arm around her shoulder and asked if she had eaten any food at all that day, then Bessie took us for a cup of tea and biscuit at the small café across the road in Dale Street.

But more importantly, my mother always recalled how Bessie spoke kindly and respectfully to her.

Incidentally, in those times things were a little different for those seeking benefit than they are today.

Our home visit from one of the hated officials of the Assistance Board resulted in a claim rejection because we literally 'had jam on the table' which was considered to be a sign of relative affluence, and therefore left my mother with two alternatives - to allow me and my sister to be put into care - or go out to work as a domestic cleaner and leave her two children aged six and seven to manage as best as they could at home. She was forced to choose the latter.

The next time I met Bessie Braddock was in May, 1960 and I was travelling back from Germany, having been discharged from National Service with the army - it was toss up who was most relieved, them or me.

I got on the train at Euston station and entered a carriage, which in those days had separate compartments.

The only other person in the compartment was a rather heavily built woman wearing a fitted coat and her trade mark black hat. Even though I was suffering from the effects of consuming half a bottle of celebration brandy, I never-the-less recognized the lady as Mrs. Elizabeth (Bessie) Braddock.

During the next 5 hours she spoke to me about working class life in Liverpool, and the problems facing those very many people, who were living in poverty, and what might be done to help them.

By the time I reached Lime Street Station, I was almost completely free of any Army indoctrination, with which I had become very slightly tinged. I never fully appreciated at that time the full significance of that conversation with the great woman, but within six months I had become somewhat more radicalised, to say the least.

I was intrigued by my introduction to working class politics, and determined to find out all I could about the subject, and more particularly how it could help to bring about change in the lives of those who were marginalised by the poverty which was the norm for so many at that time.

The next 50 years were spent trying to find out ways and means which were appropriate and I am still looking.

The third and final time that I met Mrs. Braddock was in 1968, on the steps of Saint George's Hall in Lime Street, Liverpool, with some fellow political campaigners. I was taking part in an all-night vigil and demonstration to highlight the awful situation that homeless people were facing in Liverpool every night at that time.

The idea behind it was to give a public show of solidarity with those sleeping rough, and various well-known figures amongst 'the Great and the Good' of Liverpool were invited to visit the demonstration and express their solidarity.

Surprise surprise, they did not show up - however, there was one exception, and that was Mrs. Elizabeth Braddock, MP.

This was not long before Bessie's health began to decline, but as always, she demonstrated her solidarity and concern for the least privileged in our society.

What I have attempted to show in this reminiscence, is that in fact, Bessie was an extremely kind and sensitive woman, and the pugnacious and confrontational style of her personality was reserved for those whom she considered to be causing the suffering and poverty of her beloved fellow Liverpudlians.

Needless to say she would not have gained acceptance by, or possibly even membership of, today's Labour Party.

Bessie Braddock MP.

CHAPTER FOUR

Send in the Cavalry

The Liverpool Transport Strike of 1911 and events which led up to the day known as 'Bloody Sunday', took place a few short years before the first world war. Large scale rioting, fierce confrontations between the rioters, the police and the military, resulted in injuries to many people and the loss of two lives. The industrial unrest began to build up slowly, but from June 1911, the sequence and timing of events increased, culminating in major flash points in the city during August 1911.

Eventually, the city of Liverpool was placed under martial law, and the movement of goods was severely restricted, with the City being brought almost to a standstill.

A contemporary journalist reported that the strike in Liverpool was as near to a Revolution as anything he had seen in England.

It all began with a strike of the transport workers and soon spread to other unions, who declared sympathetic strikes.

For many weeks, nothing moved in Liverpool.

The railway porters came out, the tramway men were idle. Even the road sweepers declined to work.

Troops were sent into the city, but actually increased disorder, because they were attacked by the strikers but were not allowed to fire in self-defence after the mob had armed themselves with stones.

The workers were aroused to strike by a combination of harsh work discipline, insecurity of employment, and belligerent employers with strong anti-union sentiments.

Troops and extra police were drafted in from other parts of the country.

After police were drafted in from Leeds and Birmingham, and with over 2300 troops from six different regiments camped in the city, the situation deteriorated very rapidly and matters were brought to a head on Sunday, August 13th.

A huge demonstration took place at St Georges Plateau in the centre of Liverpool and at about four p.m. a disturbance occurred when a man sitting on the window sill of the Station Hotel in Lime Street to gain a vantage point and was watching the proceedings of the meeting was ordered by the police to come down.

He refused to do so, and was brought down by the police; the huge crowd resented this, and so a fight began.

At the first sign of trouble the contingents of police emerged from the hall and baton charged the crowd.

Bystanders were attacked, and the police continued to hit men and women who had fallen to the ground, and this further antagonised the crowd.

The police repeatedly baton charged the crowd until the plateau was cleared leaving hundreds injured.

Later that day the Riot Act was read to the crowd as pitched battles took place between the police and groups of people who were looting shops and pubs.

The two deaths which occurred later during the dispute took place when troops were escorting prison vans along Vauxhall Road, en route to Walton jail, which took the prisoners through the heart of the dock area. Michael Prendergast, a docker, and John Sutcliffe, a carter, were shot dead by troops, as the prison van convoy was attacked by an angry mob.

Later a reporter from the *Daily Post*, commenting on the funeral cortege of Mr Prendergast, wrote *"The procession which passed through the streets was indeed a sad one.*

The hearse and carriages were followed by a large group

of friends and family, while immense crowds of poor people lined the streets all the way out to Ford Cemetery, on the outskirts of Liverpool."

A look at the picture on the right, would convince most people that something was very wrong, in what was then the richest country in the world,when young children in many of the poorer areas of the city were without shoes and socks. These boys are shown outside the house in Hopwood St, off Vauxhall Road, which was the home  of John Sutcliffe, who had been killed by an Army stray bullet.

The preceding image shows a cavalry troop of the Royal Scots Greys, escorting prison vans along County Road, Walton on their way to Walton Gaol after the convictions of a number of strikers for rioting.

I have often wondered how many of these troops survived the holocaust of the 1914-18 War, when the class struggle would be put on hold for the next few years while combat took place on a much bigger stage - on the battlefields of France and Belgium.

On the orders of Winston Churchill, the Home Secretary, The Government dispatched two cruisers to Liverpool Bay on the 17 August, H.M.S. Antrim was stationed in the Mersey opposite the Albert Dock, and H.M.S. Warrior was stationed in the Isle of Man at Douglas under steam, ready to enter the Mersey if the situation further deteriorated.

For what purpose it would be difficult to fathom - was Liverpool to be bombarded? Or was this a return to the policy of sending in a warship to quell the natives, whatever - the ships sailed away as mysteriously as they had arrived, a few days later.

Once the strike was over, life returned to normal and there was work for all who were able and willing to do it, clearing the buildup of shipping, and moving the goods which had piled up on the quay sides, and in the dockside warehouses.

One of the striking (pardon the pun) features of this significant episode from Liverpool's history of industrial

Armed troops escort a prison van via Scotland Road on their way to Walton Gaol

struggles was the governments intervention by the extensive use of military force in support of the police and the civil authority.

Even during the miners strike of the early eighties, the government did not include the overt use of armed military force in an Industrial dispute.

In the aftermath of the conflict, few who had witnessed the violent clashes would easily forget the bitter struggles they had witnessed. There would be many more industrial disputes in the years that followed, but thankfully none would match the bitterness and intensity of the transport strike of 1911.

CHAPTER FIVE

Bits from the Blitz

Broomfield Road bridge in Orrell Park was originally built to carry light traffic over the old Midland Railway Goods Line which connected with the Langton Dock at Seaforth.

During World War Two, if you were standing on the bridge at Broomfield Road and looking down, heavy steam locomotives could be seen hauling railway wagons carrying tanks, guns, trucks, and ammunition from the docks to British military bases throughout the UK.

Over 90% of all the war material brought into Britain from abroad, some 75 million tons, passed through Liverpool's eleven miles of quays.

This of course made the rail track a prime target for German bombers, and resulted in a number of the houses near the bridge in Kingfield Road being hit by bombs and destroyed.

Those houses were rebuilt after the war, but many of the other houses around the area had their foundations disturbed by the bombs.

On the other side of the railway tracks, just 100 metres away from the bridge at Broomfield Road is Walton Gaol. On August 19th in 1940, high-explosives fell on Walton Gaol, partially demolishing one wing and burying captives and captors alike. Twenty-one bodies were taken away by the Mortuary Service. Eleven years later, a missing body was found beneath some rubble, which was being removed from the blitzed wing of the prison.

Over 60 years later and I can still remember that night - part of the bedtime routine for small children during the blitz involved putting on what was called a siren suit before going to bed.

This was, in effect, an all in one pyjama suit, which was made of a type of rough blanket material. Its purpose was to enable parents to take their children from their beds and leave the house as quickly as possible. The signal for the evacuation of the house was the howling sound of an air raid warning siren, which indicated that a bombing air raid was about to take place.

Children of the Blitz - 1941

After putting on the children's gas masks and then hurriedly leaving the house, my mother would have had to make the choice of taking us to either a large reinforced

 concrete building, which had been constructed in the roadway of every street, or go into the Anderson shelter which was in the back garden of our house and had been buried about three feet under the surface of the garden.

Everyone was encouraged to build an Anderson Shelter in the back garden, to provide protection during air raids.

They were not built to withstand the impact of a direct bomb hit, but were designed to protect residents from the resulting collapse of the house after the bomb blast.

Inside the shelter were two wooden bunks for sleeping on, although they would be very few opportunities for anyone to sleep.

Where I lived at that time was less than a quarter of a mile from the prison at Walton, and I can clearly remember looking out at the night sky, which was a vivid red colour from all the surrounding fires, and seeing searchlights illuminating the German bombers - and of hearing the deafening noise, from the explosion of the bombs as they hit the ground.

Strangely enough I had no sense of fear, as my father in his Army Home Guard uniform with rifle on his shoulder was silhouetted in the doorway of the shelter. The next day, most people would try to resume their normal lives, or what now passed for a normal life, and would count themselves lucky just to be alive. Liverpool was the most heavily bombed area of the country outside of London, due to its importance to the UK's war effort, and the government was desperate to hide from the Germans just how much damage they had actually wreaked on the seaports, and so reports on the bombing of the area were deliberately kept low-key.

Over 4,000 Merseysiders lost their lives during the blitz, twice the number killed in Birmingham and even three times that of Coventry.

During the raid on the 12th March 1941, it is known that a force of 316 bombers were despatched against Merseyside by the Luftwaffe and a total of 303 tons of high explosive was dropped on the Liverpool Area on that one night.

Soon after Hitler came to power, Britain secretly made plans for evacuation - the moving of infants, schoolchildren, and some adults to the countryside.

In September 1940, the ship, SS *City of Benares* travelling from Liverpool to Canada with evacuated children, was sunk by a German Submarine, with the loss of 77 children and over 200 adults.

In total some 3,000 children were evacuated under the

government scheme, with around 10,000 evacuated privately.

One particularly spectacular incident occurred on May 3 when the SS *Malakand*, berthed in the Huskisson Dock, was struck by an aerial bomb which set it on fire.

Despite valiant efforts by the fire brigade to extinguish the flames, the ship's cargo of 1,000 tons of bombs exploded.

The blast destroyed the dock itself and caused a huge amount of damage to the surrounding quays.

The explosion was so violent that some pieces of the ship's hull plating were blasted into a park over a mile away.

Bootle, to the north of the city suffered the most appalling damage and loss of life. Whole swathes of streets simply disappeared, and today, street maps of the district show many grassed over areas, in an otherwise densely populated area.

One of the most vivid symbols of the Liverpool Blitz in the city is the burnt outer shell of St Luke's Church which was destroyed by an incendiary bomb on May 5, 1941.

The church was gutted, but remained standing, and still in its prominent position in the city, is a stark reminder of what Liverpool and Merseyside endured during World War Two.

Yoko Ono, the wife of former Beatle John Lennon is pictured here visiting the Peace Garden which was set up to remember all those who perished in the second world war Blitz.

It was eventually transformed into a garden of remembrance to commemorate the thousands of local men women and children who died as a result of the bombing of their city and region.

Ironically, the last German air-raid on Merseyside took place on January 10, 1942, destroying houses around the Toxteth area of Liverpool.

By one of those strange quirks of fate which history seems to often come up with, those houses which were bombed included 102 Upper Stanhope Street, had been the former home of Alois Hitler Jr., half-brother of Adolf Hitler and was the birthplace of Hitler's nephew, William Patrick Hitler.

The house was never rebuilt, and the whole site eventually cleared of housing and grassed over. But more background on that bizarre story will be found in Chapter Nineteen.

CHAPTER SIX

Take the Plane from Bootle to Speke

At the outbreak of World War II, the Royal Air Force requisitioned the airport at Speke for military use and renamed it as RAF Speke.

One of the main activities at the airport during the conflict was the construction of bomber aircraft in the factory on site.

This image shows a convoy of American aircraft being towed from the docks at Bootle, along Queens Drive and out to Speke, and was taken in June 1944. They are crossing over the junction of Rice Lane in Walton and Breeze Hill, and beginning the journey to Speke along Queens Drive. This is the junction which would eventually become The Queens Drive Flyover. Initially, deliveries of war planes to the United Kingdom from the United States were made by sea, with aircraft being put aboard ship at Long Beach, California or flown to Floyd Bennett Field in New York for partial disassembly, and then to the docks at Brooklyn and the transatlantic journey to Liverpool.

Old Speke Airport

Final assembly then took place at the new Reassembly Division of Lockheed Ltd at Speke Airport near Liverpool.

This dramatic image shows a Lockheed fighter plane passing along the Pier Head at its junction with Water Street, after being unloaded from the deck of a ship out in the river by a floating crane. It was then taken by flat bed truck, out to the Lockheed facility at Speke.

There at Speke, the aircraft facility also constructed the Handley Page, the Halifax, and Bristol Blenheim planes, and also housed the Lockheed Aircraft Corporation department.

The Lockheed group at Speke manufactured the P-51 Mustang and Hudson aircraft with the components that were shipped into Liverpool from the United States.

In 1940, the war effort increased dramatically, and Liverpool's important seaport produced a seemingly inexhaustible influx of aircraft into Speke, and then from the docks, shipped out to various overseas destinations. Inbound from the U.S.A. came thousands of American aircraft, mainly shipped into the docks and transported to the Airport at Speke for assembly. Both the Douglas Aircraft Corporation and Lockheed Aircraft Corporation used the two main hangars to assemble Mustangs and Lightning fighters.

Meanwhile in the adjacent shadow aircraft factory, the Rootes Group were producing Bristol Blenheim Bombers at a steady rate.   Speke was now overloaded with aircraft, often with over 200 planes being ready for dispatch at any one time. In 1941 Rootes Securities were awarded a contract to provide Halifax Bombers, the first Speke produced aircraft, which made its maiden flight on the 15th March,

1942.   The assembly of American aircraft continued with the types now including Thunderbolts for the USAAF and Rootes continuing to produce a stream of Beaufighters, Blenheims and Halifax Bombers.   RAF Speke is famous in wartime legends, for the fastest air to air dogfight kill during the Battle Of Britain. It is reported that

Squadron Leader Denys Gillam took to the air in his Hawker Hurricane from RAF Speke, and immediately came across a Junkers 88 aircraft passing directly in front of him. Gillam took aim and fired at the aircraft, shooting it down before the undercarriage on his Hurricane had even completely retracted. On the 18th December, 1940, No. 96 Squadron was formed purely for the defence of Merseyside, after being equipped with Hurricanes and were based not at Speke, but at Cranage, Cheshire. The defence of the City was further supplemented by two balloon Squadrons - Nos. 919 and 921 - with headquarters at RAF. Fazakerley.

This Barrage Balloon Unit, working in co-operation with the Army, also had 76 anti-aircraft guns sited around Merseyside providing large scale cover. During 1941, with numerous air-raids on the City of Liverpool, locally based Spitfires and Hurricanes were almost continuously airborne in defence of the city.

From 1944 Speke's role as a military base was run down, but the production of American types continued until the end of 1946, after which the whole Speke site was returned to civilian use.

Speke Airport Building has now become a hotel, known as The Liverpool Marriott Hotel South, and is one of the finest and most exciting hotels in the Northwest of England.

It is stunning to look at, both inside and out, with its fabulous Grade II listed art deco architecture, and very stylish contemporary surroundings.

CHAPTER SEVEN

Being an Orphan in Victorian Liverpool

Chapters: Seven, Eight, and Nine of this book cover aspects of the treatment and conditions of working class, and for that matter, some middle class Liverpool children, who grew up apart from their families in the late nineteenth century.

Starting with the poorest of the poor, this chapter takes a look at the situation of desperately poor children in Liverpool in the late Victorian period, those who were orphaned, abandoned, or in desperation chose to leave their horrific families and were forced to live on the streets.

Then in the next chapter, we consider how children lived when they were taken into care homes, or placed in establishments who would prepare them for export to one of the British colonies abroad.

And then finally, those whose families were higher up the social scale and lived in one of the many large boarding schools which existed in the City, and throughout the country, during that period.

Liverpool Society for the Prevention of Cruelty to Children

The reality behind 'Her Benny' the famous book written by the 19th-century author Silas Hocking, was that the storyline and the characters of the book were based on real situations and actual characters, and people reading the novel who were unaware of the true conditions of poor children at that time, could well be forgiven for thinking that exaggeration and poetic licence had been used for dramatic effect. In fact the author was authentically describing the social conditions of those children who were forced by circumstances beyond their control to 'live' on the streets.

Life was very different for all children during the 19th and early century, their lives were very much harder than today and discipline was rigorously applied where necessary, and also very often when unnecessary.

Extreme wealth and extreme poverty lived alongside each other in Liverpool, as it did in most other English cities, but like many other situations in life, it was very much harder for those at the bottom of the social scale.

Those who have read the book entitled *All They Need Is Love* written by Alan Brack for the Liverpool Society for the Prevention of Cruelty to Children to mark the centenary of its foundation, might find the mind numbing facts, and the shocking real-life pictures of those children in Liverpool who were unfortunate enough to be born at the end of the 19th-century, at that time and in that place, very reminiscent of the novel 'Her Benny', and would very soon realise that fact, once more, was indeed stranger than fiction.

Higher up the pecking order of depravation were the orphanages and industrial schools which had been set up to alleviate the children's plight, and were meant to ensure that they at least had food, a roof over their heads, and comparative safety from the many evils which they would otherwise be surrounded by.

From our perspective in the 21st-century, those children who were sent to live in the boarding schools and workhouse establishments of the Victorian era, could hardly be classed as fortunate.

But in comparison to the horrors of living on the streets, or in many cases, in the hellish conditions of their own homes, most of them were in fact considerably better off.

Children of the lower middle classes, whose parents were employed either as civil servants, or serving in the military and living abroad, were very often sent to one of the many boarding schools, which existed for that purpose.

One of those schools, was the Girtonville College for Young Ladies in Orrell Park, then an affluent suburb of North Liverpool.

A former pupil at the school gave the author an account of her life there, which in many ways was run in a similar fashion to

Girtonville College

the orphanages, and in some respects had almost identical aims.

Both included large groups of children who were taught their lessons, given their food and accommodation, all under the same roof.

Discipline in all of these establishments was invariably strict, and woe betide any child who did not follow the establishment rules to the letter. They all followed an almost military code of discipline which was designed to inculcate patriotism, religious conformity, and to serve dutifully in whatever capacity of employment they would eventually follow.

But let us start at the bottom of the pecking order -

One hundred years ago a quarter of the world map was coloured red, signifying the extent of the British Empire - the greatest empire the world had ever seen, and which was at its peak, with Liverpool as its second city and premier port.

It was a period which saw Liverpool's population rise to more than half a million, and soon the merchant princes began their predictable move away from the overcrowded city centre, into the cleaner air of the leafy areas to the south, and 'over the water' into Wirral. It was also a period when Liverpool despite all its wealth, had the biggest workhouse in Britain the highest infant mortality rate, with a large part of its population living at near starvation level in squalid, foul-smelling cellars, or in crumbling houses in the notorious 'courts'.

In this country at that time there was no rule whatsoever which compelled parents to provide adequate food,

clothing, or lodging for their children. A drunken parent might spend at least half his wages in the public house, and keep his children in a semi-starving and semi-neglected state, without coming under the operation of the law. Some mothers, in desperation, pleaded for their children to be admitted into custody to protect them from the violence of their drunken fathers.

The police made great use of bringing in children who had been found begging or hawking, and others who had been found wandering in the streets without a home of any kind, before the authorities.

The only place they could be put for the night was in a cell at the Bridewell, along with drunks, thieves and prostitutes. In many cases, children were forced by callous parents to stay out on the streets until well past midnight, as they knew that the later the hour and the worse the weather, the more the children would be pitied, and the more money they would get. Even young children, less than ten years old, would be forced to take a baby brother or sister with them to arouse more sympathy.

The other main offence was appearing to be neglected, which covered cases of young children being left alone  without heat or light or food for hours, or even days on end, of being allowed to roam the streets and fend for themselves in all weathers and at all hours, unwashed, ill clad and barefooted, of sick and injured children being sent out to hawk their single box of matches, or their bunch of wilted flowers.

Case histories taken at random from the files of those early years, demonstrate dramatically how life for families in Liverpool slums had degenerated to a level, which was almost unbelievable.

The squalor, the filth and the stench of their homes, derived from a struggle for survival in a world of appalling poverty and misery, which drove men and women alike to seek comfort in the only way they knew - into the pubs, and the temporary oblivion of drunkenness.

They were trapped in a vicious spiral, the worse the conditions the more they drank, the more they drank the worse they made their conditions.

Many who passed into the children's shelter were brought in by the police, who having found children begging or hawking without a licence, then arrested them and brought them to the children's shelter, before their appearance in court the next day.

Subsequently, the children were dealt with by the magistrates, along with the drunks, the thieves, and the prostitutes.

During the month of November in 1890, the NSPCC's inspectors patrolled the streets from five in the evening to seven o'clock the next morning, and reported a total of 1100 children were found to be begging on the streets of Liverpool.

Many were even without a roof over their heads, and men, women, and children alike, spent their nights huddled in shop doorways, in narrow alleyways, under arches, and on basement steps.

All the vices to which humans are prone, thrived in such squalid circumstances, and drunkenness was by far the worst, theft was close behind, and cruelty to kith and kin not far behind that.

It was a common sight to see men, women, and children, walking about the streets with their faces heavily bruised and scarred. The men bruised from fighting in drunken brawls, the women from being beaten by their men folk, and the children from being beaten by either, or both of their parents. Few thought the chastisement of a child as cruelty, let alone a crime.

As soon as a child from the slums was old enough, it was taught how to beg, and it very soon after learned how to steal. Often sent out on the streets soon after daybreak and ordered not to return until they had 'earned' by begging, or other means, a specific sum, maybe sixpence or a shilling   At the end of the first year, out of 378 cases of children being dealt with, more than 202 were ascribed to one or other parent ill treating their offspring while under the Influence of alcohol.

The other main cause was children 'appearing to be neglected'.

'Appearing to be neglected' is an official catch-all kind of description often used in those days. The reality behind the

jargon covered cases of young children being left alone without heat or light or food for hours, or even days on end - and then being allowed to roam the streets and fend for themselves in all weathers and at all hours.

They would be unwashed, ill clad, and barefooted, there were even sick and injured children being sent out to hawk their single box of matches, or their bunches of wilted violets. But things were about to change, and change for the better, and because of the changes things would never be quite so bad again.

A Liverpool businessman named Frederick Agnew travelled to New York on business in 1881, and while there, first heard the story of the formation of the American Society for the Prevention of Cruelty to Children.

The society's president told him an extraordinary story of how the society first came into being.

A lady who was visiting a poor neighbourhood in New York, found a child, whose groans and cries horrified the whole neighbourhood, the mother however, kept the child in her house under lock and key.

Applications to the police and the court were made in vain, as there was no legal redress for this situation.

So, in desperation, she addressed her complaint to the secretary for the American Society for the Prevention of Cruelty to Animals, and told them of an animal that was being barbarously treated. The society at once sent round an inspector who was completely taken aback when he found that the animal was in fact a child.

The offending mother, and her child, were brought before the courts and to the astonishment of all, the mother was convicted and punished.

At that point it was soon realised that although animals were protected by the society, and by the law, <u>children would have to be described as animals, in order to qualify.</u>

And so in America, a new society for the protection and prevention of cruelty to children came into being.

Mr Agnew returned to Liverpool later in 1882, bringing with him all the information and reportage of the American Society which he could obtain.

After many meetings in Liverpool Town Hall, and much negotiating and persuading behind the scenes, eventually in the year 1883 the formation of a society in Liverpool for the prevention of cruelty to children was achieved. Before that, the only place they could be put for the night, was in a cell at the Bridewell, along with the drunks the thieves and the prostitutes.

And so in October 1883 the very first shelter that the society opened was in Nile Street, near the Liverpool Anglican cathedral. Right from the beginning, cases of ill-treatment began to flow into the society's headquarters, imploring them to try to help or do something. The first case which the society dealt with involved a young girl who had been savagely punched in the face by her father.

The poor child was brought into court with terrible black eyes and a swollen face and the so called father was sentenced to three months imprisonment.

This caused quite a sensation, as up to that point a man would not be sent to jail for chastising his own child in his own house, such a thing was unheard of.

Thankfully, things slowly began to change for the better, and in the first year, 210 cases were brought against parents which involved cruelty to their children. If anybody had any doubt as to the needs for a society like the NSPCC, they were soon dispelled by the facts and figures when they became more widely known.

In July 1884, the newly formed Liverpool Society for the Prevention of Cruelty to Children bought a large and imposing building at 3 Islington Square in Liverpool, for the price of £1800.

This was to house the new shelter and reception facility for children brought in off the street for processing. I use the term processing, because although the primary function of the Establishment was to provide food and shelter for the children, this was only meant to be a temporary arrangement.

Prior to their arrival at Islington Square, nobody seemed to be unduly concerned about the religious affiliations of the hundreds of children wandering the streets of Liverpool each night.

However when it came to putting the children into a care home or institution, whether they were Protestant or Catholic soon became a matter of most utmost importance.

Catholic children would not be allowed to be cared for in a Protestant institution, and equally so, Protestant children would not be allowed into a Catholic one. So in a strange way, a child's religion was deemed irrelevant if the child was homeless, and would be ignored by the authorities, religious or secular.

If however the child was to be given food, shelter, education etc, till it was able to be self-sufficient, then it was considered vital that square pegs went into square holes, and round pegs went into round holes.

In Victorian Liverpool, the typical sequence of events for an abandoned or orphaned child would begin by the child being brought to the Islington Square shelter where they would be initially assessed.

Children who were brought into the shelter were usually frightened, always hungry, and usually clad only in filthy tattered clothes. They were immediately given a hot bath and washed clean with carbolic soap. Their matted hair was cut short or if it was verminous, it was cut off completely.

Their clothes were then taken away for disinfecting, or more often than not just burnt. After that, with their sores and bruises dressed, they were given a hot meal and put to bed in one of the seven large dormitories.

It would then be decided if they could be returned to their parents or whether they would be put into care at one of the institutions that existed for that purpose.

The shelter's function was basically as a holding operation, while the authorities decided what was appropriate for the child, in its particular set of circumstances.

The independent Liverpool Society continued for another 70 years to provide this lifeline, and heaven knows how many children were rescued from a life of degradation, suffering, and even death.

It was agreed in 1954, that a merger should take place between the Liverpool Society and the National Society,

and henceforth Liverpool became a regional part of the National Society for the Prevention of Cruelty to Children.

The original Children's Shelter in Islington Square Liverpool, still stands today and is currently used as a Doctors Surgery.

The Hargreaves Centre

The newly built centre in Great Homer Street Liverpool, provides therapeutic services to children and families who are affected by domestic violence, and substance and alcohol misuse.

Children and young people who have used the services feel that this is a safe place, and a haven for the children and young people of Liverpool who have suffered abuse. The building houses NSPCC services, including child protection teams that aim to protect children suffering from domestic violence, and help women who are substance users to care for their children. The Hargreaves Centre in Liverpool is the NSPCC's first customised safe haven for children. It opened in June 2007, and offers a range of groundbreaking services to children and young people all in one place.

In 2002 Merseyside police dealt with 19,500 cases of domestic violence, of which 6,176 were in Liverpool. Children are witnesses in nine out of ten cases of domestic violence in the UK and NSPCC teams work with local children, young people, and their families who have suffered from domestic violence. Staff also work with pregnant substance users, women with young children and their families. Numerous studies have made the link between drug abuse and child abuse and neglect, and child protection teams aim to protect children suffering from more domestic violence. The new building in Great Homer Street is named after the Chairman of Matalan Ltd, John Hargreaves, who launched the Safe Place Appeal in 2004 by donating over £6 million.

Although the building is now complete, significant running costs for the services still need to be raised for the NSPCC's crucial work in Merseyside to continue.   For those folk who were born after the creation of the welfare state in 1948, it would be very difficult to imagine how life in a Victorian children's institution could be seen as beneficial.

But the comparison has to be made, not with conditions as they exist today, but with the hellish conditions that were all too common for those children who were unlucky enough to be born at that time, and in that place. It would be nice to think that the necessity for having a society for the prevention of cruelty to children was no longer necessary, but sadly, the capacity still exists even today, for cruelty and child abuse in our twenty first century society.

CHAPTER EIGHT

Home, Sweet Homes

The Children's Home, or Fazakerley Cottage Homes as they were known locally, was opened in 1889 by the West Derby Board of Guardians, which was itself one of the largest Poor Law Unions in Britain, and the home had 21 separate cottages housing 584 children. On the site there were also schools, a swimming pool, farm buildings and gardens. The following is the account of an official British government report of the Fazakerley Cottage Homes in 1896.

'It is an experiment for solving one of the great social problems of the present day- the limitation of hereditary pauperism, even though its absolute prevention may not be possible'.

'Origins of the "Cottage Homes'. *The West Derby Union Workhouse had become so full from the increase of population, that additional room had to be provided for the children* somewhere else, and for a time they were accommodated in the Kirkdale Industrial Schools, by the Liverpool Parish Authorities who themselves soon began to feel the want of space. About the same time, the Dominion of Canada began to discourage the immigration of pauper children. *"The Emigration of the inmates of workhouses, or persons in receipt of parish relief is not encouraged by the Canadian Government, and this being the case, a strong desire was felt to see if the rising generation of workhouse children might not be placed under such improved conditions and training so they should become <u>worth keeping in this country</u> instead of vainly endeavouring to get them provided for in Canada, or elsewhere out of England".*

With the above object in view, the "Cottage Homes" were originated to provide in the first instance a home for the hundreds of pauper or orphan children dependent upon the West Derby Union; and secondly, to bring them up that they might be separated from their original harmful surroundings, and then they might grow up to be useful and respected, self respecting, and self-supporting members of the community, instead of perpetuating an inferior section in our midst - the class of hereditary paupers - to be a curse on themselves and a burden to others.

The provision was made of a Home with bright and healthy surroundings, instead of the inevitably depressing influence of a large workhouse.

The children were separated from all association with "pauperism," either hereditary or acquired, and were trained so that they may not be associated with what is criminal or humiliating.

All are paupers, between five and 16 years of age. The children under five years old, are left under the nursing care of their mothers if babies, or if older children, or orphans, they are in the Nursery of the West Derby Workhouse until they are five years old, when they are removed whether orphans or not, to the Cottage Homes.

CHILDRENS DORMATORY

If a single parent or a married couple enters the Workhouse with children, those above five years old are sent at once to Fazakerley, and the infants to the workhouse nursery.

On a fixed day, once a quarter, the parents of every child are permitted to go to the Cottage Homes and spend the afternoon with their children, and in the case of sickness of either parent or child, information is at once sent to the Workhouse or the Cottage Homes, and the parent or child is taken to the invalid. Thus they are mutually in the same position as the upper classes of parents, whose children have been sent to ordinary boarding or to endowed schools, except that the upper classes see their children twice or three times a year, and the inmates of the workhouse see theirs once a quarter.

The children of the Cottage Homes are of various classes, about 500 are orphans or deserted children, who are not likely to be taken out of the Homes until the age arrives (16 years as a rule) at which they must leave the "Cottages", either to enter upon life in some wage-earning capacity, or as quasi-adult paupers to be removed to the Workhouse.

Above 100 of the children have parents in the Workhouse, and they are liable to be removed at anytime; for they must be taken away when the parents leave the Workhouse.

Parents leaving the Workhouse cannot leave their children behind them in the Cottages, whatever may be their object in doing so.

About a third of the children are Roman Catholics, and they introduce a difficulty that is inevitably felt where the conflict of creeds comes into operation.

A limited number (about ten) of Roman Catholic female children have been placed under the care of the Sisters of the Nunnery at Pantasaph, near Holywell, where they are trained to be servants, and a still smaller number of Protestant girls are entrusted to a Ladies' Committee at Ambleside, who select and recommend suitable persons to receive the children into their families, so as to bring them up in actual family house life; for which 4s. per week is paid by the Guardians, and the ladies undertake to visit them regularly and see how they go on.

The girls are taught not only household work, but also sewing, knitting, darning and laundry work-and in going *through their play-rooms in the Cottages, when they were not in active play but in tranquil employment, I found one bigger girl teaching a little one how to turn the heel of the stocking that the child was knitting with its four needles, and other children doing both plain and fancy needle work.*

The latter is encouraged as a recreation and a training in something above the level of pauper life, while the former is insisted upon so far that they may be able to make all their clothing.

The boys are taught a great variety of handicrafts so as to teach them the general use of their hands, and prepare them for employment.

Theoretically, there is no corporal punishment, except under the Superintendent's inspection; but in practice, minor punishment by the cane or strap is left in the discretion of the Father or Mother, the school-master, or the workshop master; and no one who has had practical experience of a school of boys will deny the necessity and the wisdom of such discretion; keeping up, however, a careful watch that it is not allowed to merge into excess or even degenerate into cruelty.

DINING HALL

Birching, however, is a grave and very ceremonial business, and has only been resorted to on the average of 1.5 times per year since the school has been opened. (about eight times).

Birching [whipping] is a corporal punishment with a birch rod, typically applied to the recipient's bare buttocks, and occasionally to the back and/or shoulders.

It is inflicted with great ceremony by the Drill Master, in the presence of the Superintendent, and is recorded in the punishment book, which is laid before the Guardians, and is only administered for absconding from the school, inciting another boy to abscond, or for deliberate lying, or swearing or some other grave offence-and the tradition of the school is that it is "no joke."

During the first year of the Homes, birching was absolutely forbidden, but the Homes and surrounding grounds not being enclosed by walls that an average 'street arab' could not find means of scaling, it was found that a few new boys constantly revolted against the absence of freedom, and continually escaped within the first day or two, returning to their old haunts and friends.

So much so,that two special officers had to be in continual search for these waifs and strays, and it was sometimes days before they could find them.

There was no punishment that was effective - for solitary confinement, i.e. imprisonment in a cell was worse than useless with such boys, and deprivation of food only aggravated the already depressed condition of the boys morally and physically.

The Superintendent, therefore, after many fruitless endeavours, at length persuaded the Guardians to trust him with the power of the birch for absconding, or other very grievous offences; and the next little culprit in this respect was accordingly invited to an interview with him and the Drill Sergeant, and the news of its result flew like wildfire through the school; and "the master's got a rod and has flogged Tommy" was passed from mouth to mouth in hushed tones of awe.

After this, however, it was months before another boy absconded; and the knowledge of its existence has made the birch an almost unused mode of persuasion since then; and it has only been used six times during the four years of its existence.

Over a century has passed since the preceding report was written, and in these politically correct times it would be very easy to condemn the whole concept of keeping large numbers of children together in one large establishment. However, in the context of those days, and in the climate of abject poverty for those children who were unfortunate enough to be at the very bottom of the class system, it was for them without doubt a step up, but not without its own intrinsic cruelties and abuses.

It would be another 60 years before the arrival of contraception and the end of large families of unsupportable children - what Charles Dickens had termed 'the surplus population'.

The government at the time, tried many ways of dealing with it's 'surplus population'. That is where Britain's Empire, and its Colonies, came in very handy.

Britain had a booming trade in the export of its unwanted citizens to the various colonies and far-flung parts of its empire.

For orphans this was mainly to the predominantly Anglo-Saxon colonies of Canada and Australia, and in fact, the British government and its agencies continued with this policy in various guises, up until the early 1960s.

But first, the would be Australians and Canadians would need to be processed through a system that had been devised to prepare its surplus children for a useful and productive working life in their new country. The first requirement for a potential orphan/emigrant child would be its ability to meet with minimum physical requirements, as these were considered necessary in order that the child could fulfil the requirements of the host countries employers. Employment for the emigrant children had two categories - domestic service for girls, and agricultural or industrial employment for the boys.

Training Ships

There were also several reformatory ships or industrial training ships certified in the late 1850s, although they became shore-based in the 20th century.

In 1864, John Clint, a Liverpool ship owner, founded a charitable institution to train the sons of sailors, and destitute and orphaned boys, to become merchant seamen. The first was TS *Indefatigable* which was loaned by the Admiralty and was one of the last of the Navy's sailing frigates. A Mr James Bibby contributed £5,000 to transform

her from a fighting ship to a training ship in order to give maritime training to boys in poor circumstances.

There were three other training ships moored in the Mersey during the latter part of the nineteenth century. The training ship HMS *Conway*, founded in 1859, became a national institution for the training of future officers of the Merchant Navy. There were also two reformatory ships - the *Akbar*, for the reform of Protestant boys, and the *Clarence*, for Roman Catholic boys. Most of the boys from these ships were taken into the Merchant Navy. So as we can see there was a very well defined structure for dealing with children who did not fit into the accepted model of Victorian family life.

But most of those children would need to be in dire straits before they reached the required level of qualification for assistance. That still left very large proportions of families who dwelt in poverty and lived a life of desperation and misery. Real improvement in the lives of the working classes, would have to be put on hold until the end of the Second World War and the foundation of the welfare state. For all its shortcomings and inconsistencies, only a national policy, with proper funding from the government, would bring about the ending of the disgraceful inequalities and the dreadful treatment of poor working class children, which had become a scandalous hallmark of Victorian Britain.

The Liverpool Industrial School at Kirkdale

Another dubious option available for the authorities during the Victorian period was the Industrial School system, as it was called in the early days [and later known as Approved Schools]. Boys and girls under 16 who had spent time in Gaol could be transferred there. Uncertified Industrial Schools for neglected or destitute children were also opened.

These specifically juvenile institutions replaced prison terms for many young offenders, and gave boys and girls a basic education, plus a trade. The erection of this spacious building, situated in Booth Lane, Kirkdale, near Liverpool, commenced in June, 1843, and was completed at a cost of upwards of £32,000.

An official report in 1853 stated: *It was found that for some years prior to its establishment, that the juvenile pauperism of Liverpool was so largely on the increase as to be incapable of being accommodated in the workhouse. It was accordingly determined, after long and anxious debates in the vestry, that Schools should be erected at some short distance from the town, where the young children thrown upon the parish should be located apart from the adult paupers, and instructed, not only in the elements of a plain education — reading, writing, and arithmetic — and in their religious duties, but in the most common and useful trades. The institution was opened May 1, 1845, and began with 300 to 400 scholars.*

At present it contains 1123 children, of whom 640 are boys, and 483 girls; the number is limited to 1150. The trades which the boys are taught are tailoring, shoemaking, and carpentering. The girls are instructed in knitting and needlework, in washing, ironing, mangling, cooking, and general household work, so as to qualify them as domestic servants. The boys generally seem to consider it a privilege to learn to be sailors, and many of them, under the tuition thus acquired, have been qualified for, and have obtained, good situations on board ship.

No compulsion is exercised upon them as to the trade which they shall learn. It is found, that, next to the sea, the tailoring business is the most popular among them. On the day of our visit we were introduced to an assemblage of about forty young tailors, sitting cross-legged, in the approved fashion, and all being engaged, under the superintendence of a foreman, to mending clothes for the whole establishment. The labour of the female part of the establishment is turned to greater account, and the girls not only mend, but make the shirts and other articles required in the schools. The establishment, however, is admirably conducted, and is a model of order and cleanliness. The boys have an excellent band, and have made such proficiency in music as to be able to perform several favourite airs and other pieces in a very creditable manner.

The timetable was quite a strict one, the children rose at 6.00 am and went to bed at 7.00 pm. During the day there were set times for schooling, learning trades, housework, religion in the form of family worship, meal times and there was also a short time for play three times a day. In 1857 the Industrial Schools Act was passed. This gave magistrates the power to sentence children between the ages of 7 and 14 years old to a spell in one of these institutions. The act dealt with those children who were brought before the courts for vagrancy, (or in other words for being homeless).

Any child apparently under the age of fourteen found begging or receiving alms [money or goods given as charity to the poor].

Any child apparently under the age of fourteen found wandering and not having any home or visible means of support, or in company of reputed thieves.

Any child apparently under the age of twelve who, having committed an offence punishable by imprisonment or less, and any child under the age of fourteen whose parents declare him to be beyond their control.

At first the Industrial Schools were run on a voluntary basis. However the schools offered many advantages to poor children, and it became an object of ambition among many people, who are not paupers, to get their children introduced into it, in order to give them an education.

These Institutions/Schools were intended to help those

children who were destitute but who had not as yet committed any serious crime. The idea was to try and remove the child from bad influences.

Mill Apprentices at Quarry Bank Mill

With the start of industrialisation, it had become common for factory owners to employ pauper or orphaned children in their mills as "apprentices".

The 1802 Health and Morals of Apprentices Act.   This piece of legislation was the first attempt at reforming the working conditions in factories.   The Act attempted to legislate for "pauper apprentices" and fixed a maximum twelve hour working day for the children.

Other terms of the Act were:

- *Mills must have sufficient windows to ensure a flow of fresh air*
- *The walls and floor of the mill must be washed regularly*
- *Separate bedrooms must be provided for the two sexes*

- *There must be no more than two children to a bed*
- *Two suits of clothing must be provided for each child, one to be new each year*
- *For at least the first four years of their apprenticeship, children must be instructed in reading, writing and arithmetic.*
- *On Sundays, there must be at least an hour's teaching of Christianity, conducted by the local Anglican minister*

Employers breaking these regulations were to be subjected to fines ranging between £2 and £5.

Unfortunately, there were no inspectors appointed to enforce the law. Many parents were unwilling to allow their children to work in textile factories, and so to overcome this labour shortage, factory owners had to find other ways of obtaining workers. One solution to the problem was to obtain children from orphanages and workhouses, and these children became known as pauper apprentices.

This involved them signing contracts that virtually made them the property of the factory owner. One of the first factory owners to employ this system was Samuel Greg who owned the large Quarry Bank Mill at Styal in Cheshire. Greg had difficulty finding enough people to work for him. Manchester was eleven miles away, and local villages were very small. Imported workers needed cottages, and these cost about £100 each. By 1790 Greg became convinced that the best solution to his labour problem was to build an Apprentice House and to purchase children from workhouses. The building for housing the apprentices cost £300 and provided living accommodation for over 90 children.

At first the children came from local parishes such as Wilmslow and Macclesfield, but later he went as far as Liverpool and London to find these young workers.

To encourage factory owners to take workhouse children, people like Greg were paid between £2 and £4 for each child they employed.

Greg also demanded that the children were sent to him with "two shifts, two pairs of stockings and two aprons". The initial 90 children (60 girls and 30 boys) at Styal made up 50% of the total workforce. The children received their board and lodging, and two pence a week.

The younger children worked as scavengers and piecers, but after a couple of years at Styal they were allowed to become involved in spinning and carding. Eventually, some of the older boys became skilled mechanics.

The Apprentice House at Styal Mill

They worked till nine or ten at night when the water-wheel stopped.

When they stopped working, they then went to the apprentice house, about three hundred yards from the mill. It was a large stone house, surrounded by a wall, two to three yards high, with one door, which was kept locked.

The house was capable of lodging about one hundred and fifty apprentices, and with supper being the same as breakfast - onion porridge and dry oatcakes, nobody could accuse the mill owners of spoiling the children.

They all ate in the same room, and all went up a common staircase to their bed-chamber; all the boys slept in one

Apprentices House Styal Mill

chamber, all the girls in another. The bed places were a sort of crib, built in a double tier all round the chamber, and where the apprentices sometimes had to sleep two in a bed.

In the early years of the Mill, apprentices formed a substantial proportion of the Mill's workforce due to the difficulties in recruiting the necessary supply of adult labour. The earliest surviving apprentice indentures for Quarry Bank Mill date from 1785.

The Mill owners preference was to employ children from aged 9 years, despite being legally entitled to do so from aged 7, and favoured hiring girls, as it was felt that they were more obedient than boys.

The Mill's apprentices came from the parish workhouses of Staffordshire, South Cheshire, and Liverpool and some from as far afield as London and East Anglia.

Under the apprentice system, it became the factory owner's responsibility to provide food, clothes and lodging, thus relieving the pressure on parish outdoor relief, so guardians commonly made agreements with certain industrialists, satisfying the latter's need for labour, and relieving the parish of their legal responsibility for the pauper children.

Some children were also apprenticed by their parents, serving under slightly different terms to the parish apprentices, working for board and lodgings, but also with a small weekly wage. By 1790, the Apprentice House had been built to provide accommodation for the apprentices under the control of superintendents. At its height, approximately 100 apprentices lived at the House.

By modern standards, working and living conditions were harsh, but the Quarry Bank Mill owners were considered to be fair employers, providing conditions better than the norm, and in advance of legislative requirements. Discipline was strict, with punishments enforced for indiscretions, but there is no evidence of the cruelty which occurred elsewhere. It is the testimonies of runaways brought before local magistrates which has given us the insight into daily routines at the Apprentice House.

The daily regime was designed to enforce institutional life, but offered the hope that, through self-improvement, the individual could advance their status.

There are instances where an ex-apprentice has risen to the position of overlooker, and one case where an apprentice eventually became Mill Manager. Their diet was basic, but relatively plentiful for the time, with produce grown or farmed locally, some from the Kitchen Garden at the House, and tended to by the apprentices. Their health was supervised by the Mill's own physician. Unusually, for those times, there were opportunities for some to be offered employment upon completion of the indenture period.

Apprentices were provided with some basic education, and with a range of industrial skills beneficial to their future careers.

Mill records reveal that over 1,000 children served their apprenticeships at Quarry Bank Mill, many of whom continued to live and work in Styal as adults, raising their own families in the village.

Even today, there are some Styal residents who are able to trace their families back several generations to working at the Mill. By the 1820s, the cost of employing apprentices was higher than that of free labour, and the system began to lose favour nationally.

However, Quarry Bank persisted with it until the abolition of the apprentice system in 1847, no doubt due to the difficulties in obtaining sufficient supplies of external labour to keep the Mill at full productivity.

Today the Quarry Bank Mill, situated near to Manchester Airport, is part of the National Trust and is well worth a visit.

CHAPTER NINE

Girtonville College - Anyone for Tennis?

Girls in Victorian Liverpool with families who were too prosperous for elementary school, or too poor for a private governess, were usually taught by their mothers until they reached the age of nine or 10, and then were sent to a private school for a few years if they lived in one of the major cities, whilst upper middle-class families were far more likely to have a resident governess, or send them to a day school until their daughters were in their teens.

Parents who could afford private schools were very often worried about what their daughters might learn from other children. Like families who used governesses, many thought their daughter's speech, manners and standards of behaviour where more important than academic performance.

Most large communities had small private schools at that time, and the pupils were likely to be of a very similar social standing.

Typically, a widow, or a single woman who had a modest inheritance, would lease a suitable house in an appropriate neighbourhood, and might then let the women in her own social network know that she was taking in paying pupils. Her personal attention to detail and close supervision of the school pupils would be a big selling point to parents.

They believed the school was too big if it had more than twenty pupils and students. The pupils were not put into classes by their academic ability, and so, in the same class, the girls might range in age from four to fourteen.

The curriculum and teaching methods were much the same as when a private governess taught the girls at home.

The girls were not usually sent to private boarding school before their teens, unlike boys, who might leave home for boarding school, at the at the grand old age of seven or eight.

At adolescence however, girls from the middle and upper classes were often sent away to school for two or three years.

Girls' boarding schools before the last quarter of the 19th century were very similar to private day schools.

They were usually homely establishments, which were run by two or three women, who needed to support themselves independently.

The educational opportunities offered in private boarding schools depended entirely on the proprietors personal interests and their educational abilities.

Some establishments provided a first-class instruction in foreign languages, while others would place the emphasis on culture, social graces and personal appearance.

These houses at the corner of Warbreck Road in Orrell Park, Liverpool, were built on the site of the former Girtonville College for Young Ladies.

This was destroyed by an aerial landmine which was dropped during the May blitz of 1941.

Fortunately, the building was empty that night - apart from an air raid warden who was killed by the blast. The author remembers hearing that the unfortunate man's severed head, with steel helmet still attached, was found the next day at Orrell Park Station, 300 yards away.

Girtonville College for Young Ladies was situated at the corner of Warbreck Road and Orrell Lane in the Walton area of North Liverpool and was a private school for young ladies. It was situated in a very large building with a conservatory and a large garden. The school was run by a Mrs Swan Johnston and her sister.

The dormitories and living quarters for the staff and pupils were in a separate house opposite the college.

The author was recently at a local history gathering and was about to deliver a lecture featuring Girtonville College, describing the college's background, and mentioned to the audience that he thought it very unlikely that any of them would have heard of it, as it had been destroyed during the Second World War in the May Blitz on Liverpool.

To his surprise an elderly lady informed him that, not only had she heard of it, but had attended the school as a pupil for some years shortly after the first world war.

In a later interview in April 2008 with a former pupil of the college - Miss Franklin Corris, he learned that Miss Corris attended the Girtonville College in Orrell Park in 1922, a small private school for boys and girls.

The strongest memories of her time at the school were the dancing lessons on a Friday afternoon, which took place on the lawn in the summer and in the main hall during the winter. Miss Corris said, she began learning to paint in watercolours at Girtonville College and later in life, she exhibited her work at various exhibitions in London.

Girtonville College was a general educational establishment, although there were boarders accommodated in a large house on the opposite side of Orrell Lane.

Their parents would be working in various parts of what was then Britain's overseas Empire, and their children would usually be placed as boarders at a school somewhere in England.

Oakes Institute - Situated at the far end of Sefton Road, off Rice Lane. The school was founded in 1919 to provide higher education for boys in the northern end of Liverpool, by the Liverpool Education Committee, under the chairmanship of

James W. Alsop, after whom the school was named (Queen Mary High School for girls was founded at the same time.)

The school was originally spread around several locations - an existing private school called the Oakes's Institute, the Brook Road Methodist Sunday school, the Aintree Institute and Longmoor Lane School were all

once part of the fledgling Alsop High School - they must have had a great time going between classes

The Oakes Institute, a private school owned by a Mr. Oakes and operating in the Aintree area, was eventually taken over and a new building on Queen's Drive was built to replace the various classrooms scattered about Rice Lane and Walton Vale. The new establishment became known as Alsop High School for Boys.

The previous sections in chapters: seven, eight, and nine have attempted to illustrate how differently orphaned and abandoned children were treated during the affluent period of the 19th and 20th centuries.

Any right thinking person today would be horrified by the plight of those poor children who inhabited the bottom layer of society, not only in Liverpool, but throughout the length and breadth of Britain.

Probably the most shocking aspect of their situation was the fact that it took place during that period, when Liverpool, the so-called second city of the empire, possessed such an abundance of wealth. However, once the children left the streets and entered into the institutional system their lives did change, and for the majority of them, because of their previous hellish experiences, this meant that overall it would mostly be for the better. The government's policy for children in care was to provide huge institutions, which very often accommodated up to a thousand children at any one time. This was continued up until the early nineteen sixties, and the arrival of the contraceptive pill, with subsequent massive reductions in the numbers of unwanted children.

Although far from ideal, the situation for orphaned and destitute children in Victorian Britain, when compared with today's abandoned children who live in the developing world, was probably the best that could be done under the circumstances and the social attitudes of those times.

CHAPTER TEN

The Aftermath of a Mutiny

Grace Lodge is a residential nursing home situated in Grace Road, off Walton Vale, a quiet and peaceful home for elderly people.

Before the first World War, a factory occupied the site, which had been built in 1912 for the mass production of false teeth, and was later converted during the War into an Army Barracks.

It was to be the scene of one of Liverpool's many strange, and often little known episodes of history, many of which had national, and even international significance. This unusual story concerns the fifty-one Canadian soldiers who were court-martialled at Grace Road Barracks for Mutiny, as a result of their alleged roles in the Kinmel Park Mutiny, which took place at an Army Camp in St Asaph, North Wales, during March 1919. In the six months after the ending of the first World War, between November 1918 and June 1919, there were thirteen instances of disturbances involving Canadian troops in England.

During the early part of 1919 however, there were over 100 disturbances involving about 100,000 troops of the

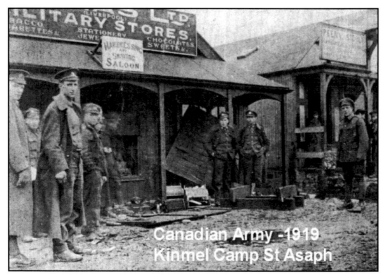

Canadian Army -1919
Kinmel Camp St Asaph

British Army who were demanding that demobilisation be speeded up.

The scene was set, the pressure was increased, and something had to give.

148th "OVERSEAS" BATTALION
CANADIAN EXPEDITIONARY FORCE
Headquarters:
435 SHERBROOKE ST. WEST, MONTREAL

Will You and Your Friends
— Come Overseas ? —
IF SO SEND US ONE OF YOUR BEST MEN NOW TO BE TRAINED AS A N.C.O. BAYONET FIGHTER OR PHYSICAL INSTRUCTOR.

Come and be Together and Make Your Home Town Proud of You.

Rates of Pay
Sergeants $1.35 $2.25 $25.00
Corporals . . . . 1.10   .10   20.00
Lance Corporals . . . . 1.05   .10   20.00
Privates . . . . 1.00   .10   20.00
PAY, FIELD AND SEPARATION ALLOWANCES START FROM DAY OF ENLISTMENT.

A. A. MAGEE, Lt.-Col.
Commanding Officer

One of the many points of pressure was the 20,000 Canadian troops billeted at Kinmel Camp and who were waiting for transport to take them back to Canada after an absence of over four years fighting with the Allies in France.

Daily existence for the soldiers at Kinmel Park while awaiting passage home to Canada, was generally cold, uncomfortable, and monotonous. The men persistently complained about overcrowding, insufficient and badly prepared food, shortage of fuel, insufficient blankets and delays in pay. This was further increased by a succession of delays and postponements of Canadian bound shipping, departure dates with frequent postponements by the Ministry of Shipping, and sailing dates which were published but did not take place.

In February more sailings were cancelled because of vessels requiring repairs, and British ship owners who were unable to carry out the work because of striking shipyard workers.

When it became known that three large ocean liners, which had already been allocated for Canadian troops, the *Mauritania*, the *Aquitania*, and the *Olympic*, and due to sail from Liverpool, had been re-allocated for the use of American troops, the grumbling soon developed into an organised protest.

On Tuesday, 4th March, 1919, rumours of impending trouble circulated the camp throughout the day; apparently, the trouble began in the Army's canteen when about 20 of the soldiers refused an order from the Military Police to leave. Word began to spread around the camp and other men soon began to join in, they approached other canteens, of which there were quite a number, and within about 15 minutes a 200 strong crowd began to attack the officers' mess. The premises were ravaged, stock was looted, and furniture had been smashed by the time that a party of military police reached the centre of the camp. There, they were met by a small band of loyal soldiers who had been unable to prevent the pillage and looting which had been carried out. The officer commanding the camp ordered out a cavalry detachment and thought perhaps 60 – 70 mounted troops would be able to disperse the crowd.

The Commanding Officer of the camp tried to talk to the raiders but soon discovered many of them were too drunk and too angry about the issues of no pay, no sailings, and no tobacco, to listen.

Meanwhile, the cavalrymen seemed reluctant to attack the rioters, and so in the end the officer in charge decided it would be useless to try to convince his men of the need to do so.

Many of the crowd had decided to try to release the prisoners, who were held in the camp guardroom, and did finally manage to release eight of the prisoners.

In fact, the riot or mutiny, was essentially a looting of the shops and canteens, where the men proceeded to drink as much as they could lay their hands on. As dawn broke on 5th March, the damage to the camp was now very apparent.

Eleven of the shops, which sold food and other items used by the troops, had been wrecked and stripped of their contents, the soldier's mess, where they ate and drank had been looted, two of the YMCA buildings had been attacked, and the quartermaster's stores where they kept tobacco and alcohol, had been broken into and robbed.

Thousands of pounds worth of food, drink, and tobacco had been stolen or destroyed, and the churned up ground was littered with broken debris from the buildings that had been wrecked in the process.

It soon became clear that the mutineers were intent upon

releasing more of their comrades, those who had been captured and imprisoned on the previous day.

The situation then began to change dramatically with the arrival of troops from other regiments, who were fully armed and proceeded to mount a series of raids upon the areas controlled by the mutineers.

There could only be one winner in the ensuing conflict, as it became a battle between the mutineers with sticks and stones, and those troops who had remained loyal, and had been organised into raiding parties after being issued with rifles, ammunition, and bayonets.

In this final showdown, the human toll of the eighteen hour struggle began to emerge.

Two of the rioters had been bayoneted to death and three others died as a result of gunfire. There were twenty-eight other casualties with a variety of injuries and who were treated in the camp hospital.

One can only imagine the bitterness and frustration felt by the Canadian troops after having spent four years, and had given so many lives to the British war effort. The situation that the British government found itself in at the end of the First World War caused a number of simultaneous crises which were to have a profound effect on what happened at Kinmel Park. The nationwide industrial discontent caused by increases in the cost of living, poor housing, and excessively long hours of work, exploded in a wave of strikes by shipbuilding, engineering and transport workers. Further pressure on the government came from the IRAs renewed campaign to end the British occupation of Ireland.

The UK government's power was almost fully stretched and barely coping with the many demands upon its resources, and as if that was not enough, the opening weeks of the New Year of 1919 witnessed a strike by British policeman, at a time when a wave of strikes were sweeping across the British Isles.

On Wednesday 5th March 1919, fifty eight of those who had been arrested and imprisoned in the camp guardroom at Kinmel Camp were taken to cells at Walton Gaol in Liverpool, where they would await the court martial, which was to be held in the nearest local army camp.

The first of the hearings took place on 6 April 1919 at Grace Road Barracks, off Walton Vale. But how British and Canadian soldiers ended up shooting their own comrades in anger still raises many unanswered questions.

The trial failed to unearth any revolutionary conspiracies in the defendant's ranks, but there remains a stench of injustice about the manner in which these Canadian soldiers were apprehended, and then punished.

Eyewitnesses who might have contradicted some of the statements made by the prosecution did not appear, because some of them had already been shipped to Canada and demobilised.

Thanks to the diligence of the defending officers, a total of seventeen defendants were acquitted before the final hearing on 6 June.

The remaining men were found guilty of joining the mutiny, and of attacking officers, damaging buildings, and resisting arrest.

The ringleaders were among those convicted, and the sentences awarded by the court ranged between seven and ten years of penal servitude. Rather surprisingly, their war service and sufferings in France did not appear to lessen their sentences.

A particularly severe sentence was passed upon another Canadian veteran, Private John Brennan, who had been three times wounded in France. He was convicted of participating in the mutiny, and was given one year's imprisonment with hard labour.

Nobody was ever tried for the five deaths which occurred, but one of the officers who had been involved in the conflict at Kinmel was reminded later when they were back in Canada by some of the veterans about his role in the trials. The officer, was recognized by a couple of former soldiers, who gave him the beating of his life.

It is probably best summed up by the words of one of the Canadian veterans, who concluded that:

"We just wanted to be treated like men, we wanted to know that someone was dammed well looking after us. We got none of that. You can put the riot down to one thing - lack of concern for the men by the higher ups, an officer's job is to look after his men irrespective of the conditions, well we had a lot of lousy officers."

Over the years the stories that have been told and retold of the Kinmel Park riots, probably have only a tenuous link with the truth.

For a long time it was believed that some of the Canadians had been executed for their role in the mutiny and then buried in the churchyard at St Asaph. This is considered by most historians as unlikely - but in fact we will probably never know the full story.

St Asaph Church

For those wishing to read more of the events which took place at Kinmel in 1919, an excellent account of what happened is available from the Flintshire Historical Society - it is entitled *The Kinmel Park Riots 1919* and written by the military historian, Julian Putkowski. An interesting footnote to this story may appeal to those who belong to the 'conspiracy theory' school of opinion There was a reluctance by the Allies to demobilise too quickly after the Armistice of 1918. In Britain after the war there was considerable tension and a fear that law and order might break down in the big cities. Had this happened in one of the potential trouble spots like Glasgow, Manchester or Liverpool, Canadian troops might well have been sent in to restore order. A police strike had already taken place during 1919, and in Russia there had been a complete overthrow of the government during the Bolshevik Revolution.

In the aftermath of a major war there could be great civil unrest, with soldiers returning to the relative calm and peace of civilian life without having, in effect, been exorcised from their previous occupation of killing and violence.

We now recognize that a major conflict, and the effects of

demobilisation can cause major changes in society. In order to control civil unrest it is necessary for the government to have a force which could be relied on to remain loyal to the government. The Canadian Army would be seen as eminently suitable for that role. It is most likely that financial considerations were at the top of the list of priorities for those in authority, and was one of reasons why ships were not available.

Neither the British nor the Canadian Governments, had ownership of the vessels that were needed for the transportation of the troops back to Canada, and American military interests ensured that their troops would be given priority in the race to get their men shipped back home across the Atlantic. Having 200,000 men who had been away from home for four years fighting in the bloodiest war in history, and based in an isolated camp in rural Wales with poor food and very little entertainment, was asking for trouble.

It was very predictable that the unrest eventually turned into mutiny, and the mutiny resulted in death and severe injuries.

What is remarkable, is that there were not many more casualties.

CHAPTER ELEVEN

Two Titanic Stories

Henry Tingle Wilde was born on the 21 September 1872 in Walton, Liverpool, England and was later christened at the Loxley Congregational Chapel in Bradfield, Yorkshire on the 24 Oct 1872.

He was the son of Henry Wilde, and Elizabeth Tingle, who came originally from Ecclesfield in South Yorkshire.

His parents moved home soon after their marriage to live in Highfield Road, Walton in Liverpool, where Henry Wilde, senior, practised his profession as an Insurance Surveyor.

The young Henry Wilde decided from an early age on a career in the Merchant Navy as a Deck Officer. He went to sea in his early teens and became apprenticed as an Officer with a local shipping company, James Chambers & Co., Liverpool, with whom he served on board various sailing ships, including the *Greystoke Castle* and the *Hornsby Castle*. His first steamship posting was the S.S. *Brunswick* in 1895, on which he served initially as third mate, and then as second mate. In July 1897, he joined the White Star Line, starting as a junior officer. Henry Wilde's career began to flourish as he rose steadily through the ranks while serving on several different White Star ships.

Henry Tingle Wilde married Mary Catherine Jones around 1892/3, and the couple had 6 children. The family lived in 25 Grey Road, a modest terraced house off Rice Lane, in the Walton area of north Liverpool. A terrible tragedy struck the Wilde family soon after Mrs Wilde gave birth to twin boys on 19th November 1910, when one of the twins died on  the 2nd December 1910, and was buried on the same day, and then the second child died a few days later.

As if they had not suffered enough already, further tragedy struck shortly after the death of the twin boys. Their mother was to go the grave herself on 24th December 1910, leaving Henry Wilde to bring up their remaining four children by himself.

After putting the four remaining children into the care of relatives, Mr Wilde decided to resume in his chosen profession as Master Mariner and continued to sail with the White Star Line.

He was an old friend of Commodore Edward John Smith, Captain Smith who when not at sea, resided at 17, Marine Crescent, Waterloo, Liverpool

At that time Captain Smith was White Star's highest paid Captain, and although due to retire, Captain Smith was persuaded to command the Titanic on her maiden voyage, as a fitting finale to a glittering career.

Henry T Wilde was asked by Captain Smith if he would take the post of Acting Chief Officer, and he accepted - so becoming a last minute substitute for another colleague.

Almost at the last minute, Wilde signed on to the *Titanic* on 9 April, 1912 and reported for duty at 6 am on 10 April, on the day of sailing.

When Captain Smith came aboard at about 7.30 am, he received sailing reports from all his senior officers. Wilde reported the condition of equipment, stores and the readiness of public areas and staterooms.

Captain Edward John Smith and some of the crew of the 'Olympic'
Left to Right: William McMaster Murdoch, Charles A. Bartlett, Henry Tingle Wilde and Captain Edward John Smith

In a letter to his sister, posted at Queenstown, Wilde gave some indication that he had misgivings about the new ship: *"I still don't like this ship... I have a queer feeling about it"*. Nonetheless things began relatively smoothly for a maiden crossing. At 2 pm on 14 April, he relieved William Murdoch on the bridge, perhaps they may have discussed the proximity of ice. About a quarter of an hour beforehand, the SS *Baltic* had transmitted an ice warning telling of icebergs in the path of the *Titanic*.

Tragedy struck the ship when it hit an iceberg floating in the Atlantic, just off the coast of Newfoundland, and the huge vessel slowly began to sink. About 1.30 am he ordered Lowe to take command of lifeboat 14.

Around this time, Mr Wilde interrupted Officer Lightoller to ask where the firearms were kept. When Lightoller had been first officer at Southampton these had been his responsibility. Lightoller did not understand why Wilde wanted the guns but he led Wilde, Captain Smith and First Officer William Murdoch to the locker in the First Officer's cabin.

As Lightoller was about to leave Wilde shoved a revolver in his hand with some ammunition saying *"Here you are, you may need it"*. Wilde had been described as having a "powerful" look.

According to a witness, Wilde single handedly drove out a group of firemen and stokers who were trying to get into a boat.

The crowds began to press in and Lightoller now realized why Wilde had asked him for the guns.

First Officer Wilde drew his pistol and called on the crew to put a ring of men around the boat - things were now getting desperate. Wilde waited as long as he could, but it was clear that the ship was nearing the end.

Through sheer force of personality, Wilde prevented panic aboard the Titanic and supervised the loading of the lifeboats, saving many lives in the process.

A Tragedy of Titanic Proportions

Artists Impression

What is certain is that he worked diligently to load the boats once the seriousness of the situation was made clear to him.

Wilde told Lightoller to get aboard but the Second Officer refused, and jumped out of the boat before it was lowered the short distance to the water. Witnesses reported at the inquiry, that Henry Wilde was last seen trying to free some of the collapsible lifeboats which were jammed on the roof of the officers' quarters. Mr Wilde was one of the 1500 people, passengers and crew, who perished in the freezing waters, and his body, if recovered, was never identified. His family was later to receive some financial relief from the fund which had been set up for the survivors and relatives of those who perished in the disaster.

The story of Mr and Mrs Wilde and their children is a series of tragedies - the untimely early death of Mrs Wilde, so soon after childbirth and following the death of their twin boys within weeks, would be considered tragic enough, although in the early twentieth century such events were sadly, not uncommon. The spectacular events in the icy waters of the North Atlantic, which took place less than two years later, completed the Wilde family's tragic history, and became one of the *Titanic*'s saddest of many sad tales.   Mr Wilde is remembered on a memorial beside the family grave in Kirkdale Cemetery, Longmoor Lane, Fazakerley, Liverpool.

The inscription on the memorial at Kirkdale cemetery reads:

> '*Captain Henry T. Wilde, RNR*
> *Acting Chief Officer*
> *Who Met His Death in the SS*
> *Titanic Disaster*
> *15th April 1912 aged 38 years.*
> *"One of Britain's Heroes"*

The Port of Liverpool, and the White Star Line, later commissioned a Titanic memorial to remember the heroism

and devotion to duty shown by the ship's engineers, who remained at their posts operating electrical and pumping equipment to ensure that the ship stayed afloat for as long as was possible.

It stands in a very prominent position adjacent to the Liver Insurance Building, and looks out across the wide expanse of the River Mersey, and towards the landing stage where once the biggest of the White Star and Cunard liners would tie-up, ready to embark expectant passengers travelling to the New World. It bears the following inscription:

IN HONOUR OF ALL THE HEROES OF THE MARINE
ENGINE ROOM THIS MEMORIAL WAS ERECTED BY
INTERNATIONAL SUBSCRIPTION MCMXVI'

Another fitting memorial is dedicated to the *Titanic*'s band and is to be found on a carved plaque located at Liverpool's Philharmonic Hall, it reads:

MEMBERS OF THE BAND ON BOARD THE "TITANIC";
THEY BRAVELY CONTINUED PLAYING TO SOOTHE
THE ANGUISH OF THEIR FELLOW PASSENGERS
UNTIL THE SHIP SANK IN THE DEEP ON APRIL
14TH 1912. 'COURAGE AND COMPASSION JOINED
TOGETHER MAKE THE
HERO AND THE MAN COMPLETE.

An eye witness account given to the *New York Times* by one of the survivors - ship's baker Walter Belford said *"We were working on the fifth deck amidships, baking for the next day. There was a shudder all through the ship about 11.40 pm. The provisions came tumbling down and the oven doors came open. I escaped by going down the side of the ship from a rope just before she sank."* Mr Belford said one of his most vivid recollections was the sight of Captain Smith standing resolutely on the bridge as the ship went down.

He quoted Smith as he addressed a group of remaining crewmen after the last boats were gone, *"Well boys, I've done the best I can for you. Now it's in your own hands. Do the best you can to save yourselves."* Belford continued, *"We went over to the side straight away, I jumped overboard from the well deck about thirty feet above the water."* He was wearing his white baker's uniform and a life jacket with a quart of whiskey stuck in his belt. Five hours later he was rescued from the bone-chilling water. *"I kept taking a sip of whiskey from time to time to keep warm. There were a couple of shots left when I was rescued."*

"Why on earth did the ship hit the iceberg when it had received four warnings during the day, five warnings really, although the last one might not have gotten to the captain". The *New York Times*, on the Sunday after she had hit the iceberg, was full of stories about icebergs in the north Atlantic, and the stories were all over the paper - why on earth did this great ocean liner plunge into the midst of all those icebergs without slowing down? The vessel was designed to forsake speed in order to achieve increased safety and comfort. The many millionaire passengers might grab the newspaper headlines, but the vastly increased capacity for the third class emigrant passengers, as well as more accommodation for the middle classes, would make the vessel economically successful, and, of course, more profitable.

This is the last known photograph of the Titanic, taken as she left Queenstown (Cobh) in Ireland, to begin her maiden and final voyage across the Atlantic to New York.

Titanic Story of a Gentleman

One of the many tragic stories that emerged after the sinking of the Titanic is the true story of 'The Two Gold Watches'.

It begins in 1902 when newly married young couple Tom and Ada Hewitt gave to each other gold pendant watches as wedding presents.

Tom was to remember this romantic event ten years later, when he faced almost certain death, as the *Titanic* began to sink on that fateful night in April.

Thomas Hewitt was a crew member who sailed with the Liverpool shipping company - the White Star Line. The first part of the journey from home to his ship would usually involve taking the steam train from Orrell Park station into Liverpool city centre, and each time he was accompanied to the station by his wife Ada, and their son and daughter.

The family lived in a modest terraced house opposite to Kingfield Gardens in Devonfield Road, in the Orrell Park area of Liverpool.

Taking his last train journey from Orrell Park Station on his way to join up with the *Titanic* on its maiden voyage, Tom waved to his family from the carriage window of the train until he was out of sight. After the disaster, Ada often wondered whether or not it was a premonition that prompted him to wave farewell, as it was the only time he had ever done so – maybe he did, who knows?

Tom was one of the *Titanic*'s crew members who joined the ship at Belfast, as part of the small team which took the new vessel from there to Southampton, where, after picking up its passengers, its coal and its supplies, the ship's maiden voyage to New York was to due to begin on April 10th 1912.

On the evening of 14th April, with over two thirds of her journey completed, disaster struck the RMS *Titanic*, in the form of a collision with a massive iceberg.

All male members of the crew were expected to remain at their posts in order that passengers (women and children first!) could enter the lifeboats safely.

As a last gesture, before facing his almost certain death, Tom Hewitt asked one of the female bedroom stewards if she would take his gold pendant watch, and if she did manage to survive, to try to return it to his wife Ada, back at home in Orrell Park, Liverpool.

The unnamed stewardess did manage to survive and she kept her word, and in due course she kept her pledge and managed to return the watch to Mrs Ada Hewitt and her children in Liverpool.

When the *Titanic* sank, at 11:40 pm, Tom Hewitt was one of over 1500 people who lost their lives.

Of a total of 2,223 people on board the ship, only 706 survived; and over 1,500 perished.

The majority of deaths were caused by hypothermia in the freezing waters of the North Atlantic (-2 °C). Tom's body was recovered later, but Ada was now a widow with two children to raise, and could not afford to have him shipped back to Liverpool for burial.

He is believed to be buried in Halifax, Nova Scotia (on the east coast of Canada). The gold watch was later donated by the family to Liverpool Maritime Museum, and is one of their many Titanic related artifacts. There are many other fascinating accounts of the Titanic, but the stories of Henry Tingle Wilde and Thomas Hewitt are notable because although they lived within a mile of each other, one was an Officer and second in command of the ship, while the other was an ordinary seaman.

Both were, however, extraordinary in sharing exemplary courage, and in their heroic deaths.

Author's note: I am reminded of this fascinating story

every time I pass their former residence, which is situated just around the corner from where I live.

The sinking of the *Titanic*, A Love Story, Heroism and Tragedy, all the ingredients for a blockbuster novel are contained just below the surface of this ordinary Liverpool suburban street.

Just one more example of how often fact can sometimes be far stranger than fiction.

The sinking of the *Titanic* and all the speculation which has always surrounded the tragedy, has long been a subject of international historical interest and remains so to this day.

The epic events which took place in the north Atlantic Ocean in April 1912 have been the subject of countless books and newspaper articles, television documentaries and full length films, public enquiries and all the usual conspiracy theories.

As in most cases though, the whole subject takes on more relevance when a personal link, however remote, enables the observer to identify with the subject. Even though maritime disasters were much more commonplace then, with many thousands of ships sunk during both World Wars, the sinking of the *Titanic* has resulted in an abiding interest and fascination with all the events and people involved, and is likely to remain so in the future.

CHAPTER TWELVE

Two Very Curious Murders

Murder at the Old Curiosity Shop

On the site of what is now the BP Petrol Station, at the junction of Hall Lane, Albany Road, and Warbreck Moor, there had previously stood a 16 room Victorian house which was known locally as 'The Old Curiosity Shop'. Every room on the ground floor of the house was crammed full of memorabilia and junk of every kind.

It was to be the scene of the dreadful murder in January 1953 of its 86 year old owner George Walker, who lived alone there. The owner of the Old Curiosity Shop, Mr Walker, was a small, frail, 82-year-old retired tailor who lived there alone, with only his two dogs for company.

On the evening of the 15th of January 1953, one of the neighbours, who had been alarmed by the incessant barking of dogs from the house, began to realise that something was wrong and rang the police on 999.

The police eventually had to force their way into the house and there on the floor of the hallway was the bloodstained body of Mr Walker, who appeared to have been dead for some time.

A murder enquiry was immediately set up, and the police began the hunt for the person, or persons, responsible.

If this crime had taken place now, it would not have caused anything like so much interest in the grisly event, but because such crimes of violence, especially of murder, were extremely rare, the murder at the old curiosity shop became the subject of intense speculation in the city, and especially in the area of North Liverpool.

A local man had been seen calling on Mr Walker from time to time, and had expressed an interest in Mr Walker's old clocks and watches, and he would frequently offer to help Mr Walker to keep the place tidy.

Eventually, the police, after taking almost 14,000 statements, managed to arrest a local man, known as John Lawrence Todd, who lived with his mother at 98 Roxburgh Street in Walton.

Todd had been employed as a part time cinema attendant at the Bedford Cinema in Bedford Road, Walton, and his girlfriend, who was also one of the usherettes at the cinema, was a woman by the name of Iris Tucker, who lived nearby, in Bootle.

After reading the details of the horrific murder, and the description of the suspect in the local paper, Miss Tucker was convinced that the description of the man the police were looking for fitted her boyfriend John Todd, she was also aware of Todd's recent visits to the house in Warbreck Moor, known locally as 'the old curiosity shop'.

The suspicion that Todd was in fact the man the police wanted to question for the murder, was sufficient for Iris Tucker and her father to report the matter to the police. Todd was arrested at his house in Roxburgh Street and was then taken to Rice Lane police station for questioning, and where he was then charged with Mr Walker's murder. The accused, after a three-day hearing was committed for trial at the Crown Court, in April 1953, which was held, at that time, in St George's Hall. John Todd pleaded not guilty, but the evidence submitted by the prosecution proved to be too strong, and inevitably the jury returned a guilty verdict. In those times, Capital Punishment was normally applied in nearly all cases of murder, and when the judge had finished summing up he pronounced sentence on the accused. Before the death sentence was pronounced, the judge would put on his head a black square of silk known as 'the black cap'.

WALTON PRISON

The sentence of death by hanging was carried out on John Todd at Walton Prison, at 9am on the 19th of May 1953, for the murder of Mr

Walker. Although the surrounding buildings have remained unchanged, the old curiosity shop was demolished many years ago, and a petrol filling station now stands on the site.

The Vanishing Credit Draper

Harry Baker - Deceased

This almost forgotten story tells of a strange crime incident which took place in Bootle just over 50 years ago, and which involved the robbery and murder of an elderly credit draper.

In the late afternoon of June 6th in 1958, a rather small elderly gentleman was seen to wave goodbye to a woman standing at the door of a terraced house in Strand Road, in Bootle.

The old gentleman concerned was Harry Baker, a 61-year-old Jewish credit draper from Southport, or 'the club man' as they were known at that time. Mr Baker was making his usual round of collections from his housewife customers in the Marsh Lane/Strand Road area of Bootle.

In those days, before the arrival of the ubiquitous credit card, and store credit, the credit draper enabled people without cash to purchase just about anything, though usually with quite a high rate of interest.

It was claimed that this high interest was necessary to offset the frequent non-payment of monies owed.

The credit draper, a kind of travelling salesman, who peddled goods for credit on behalf of large warehouses, and customers, especially women, would order goods of all kinds through a credit draper who would deliver the goods, and then be re-paid by weekly instalments.

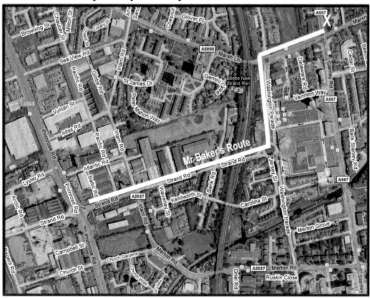

However, Friday June 6 in 1958 was a collection day with a tragic difference for mild-mannered Harry - 'a friendly little gent' is how one of his customers described him - the debt collector who never pushed his customers too hard if they could not pay. Mr Baker set off from Strand Road on his way to visit the next customer on his list. He continued along Marsh Lane to the junction known as Parr's Corner, and then disappeared into Stanley Road, in the general direction of Linacre Lane.

He was never to be seen again alive.

Parr's Corner - Marsh Lane

After Harry Baker failed to return to his home in Southport that night, the police were alerted by his family, as he always returned to his home as soon as his working day ended.

Despite frantic searches to try and discover his whereabouts, no trace of him could be found.

Nearly three weeks later, Mr Baker's battered body was discovered behind a hedge at the junction of the A50 and the A556, at a spot known as Mere Corner.

Despite a huge police investigation involving over 25,000 interviews and the offer of a sizable reward for information leading to the conviction of Mr Baker's killer, the police remained baffled by the crime.

All that could be positively established was his identity, the date of his disappearance, and the place were the corpse was discovered.

The police at the Bootle Police HQ, in the days before the force was amalgamated into the new Merseyside Police, were forced to file the case away as an unsolved crime, and it remains so over fifty years later.

Many years have passed since the murder of Harry Baker and in all that time, no clues to identify the killer, or killers, nor further witnesses to any of the events before or after Mr Baker's death have emerged.

They are the basic facts about the case.

In late July of 1958, a young soldier was hitch-hiking in uniform, as was the case in those days, back home to Liverpool from his military base in Tidworth, in Wiltshire.

It had been a difficult and tiring journey, sometimes he was quite lucky in getting good lifts, but not this time, as his journey had followed a zigzag, cross country pattern, rather than a more direct route.

He set off from his army camp in the late afternoon, and by 3am next morning, had managed to reach a point, just north of Knutsford, on the A50 trunk road.

The motorist who had kindly provided him with the lift, needed to take the right fork for Manchester, the A556, at the road junction known as Mere Corner.

The soldier got out of the car, as he needed to stay with the A50 road towards Warrington and on to Liverpool. The time was now after 3am, and it was almost completely pitch black.

After waiting for about 15 minutes the serviceman was feeling really tired, and hoping for the next car headlights to appear soon. The wait seemed to be never ending, as is often the case.

He eventually turned to look at what was behind him, and to his considerable surprise noticed that a rather strange looking man was standing in a field behind a hedge, about 10 feet back from the roadside and not saying a word, but looking directly at him. The man had a slightly vacant look, but made no sound, and did not attempt to speak.

The fact that anybody would be standing behind a hedge in such a secluded place was extremely strange, to say the least, but it never occurred to the soldier to say anything or to question why he was standing there.   The next thing that he could remember seeing was a car's headlights in the distance, about a mile away, coming towards him.   What was probably uppermost in the man's mind at that time, was just to get a lift, and then to continue on his journey home.

But to his surprise, when the car pulled up it turned out to be a police patrol car, and one of the two officers inside began to ask him questions. They asked him what he was doing there, had he seen anything suspicious, and where he had been recently.

He told the police that he was hitch-hiking home on leave from the Army, and that he had spent the last eight weeks in Catterick Military Training Camp in North Yorkshire.

"Well," said one of the officers. *"You will not get a lift where you are standing, because in the field behind the hedge, a murder victim's body was found last week."*

Although the soldier had only been in the Army a matter of a few months, he had already learned not to volunteer, or to answer questions, other than just giving the most basic information.

Then of course came the inevitable question, *"Show me your leave pass"*.

Well, of course he didn't have one. *"We will have to take you to the station for checking,"* one said. The other replied, *"Oh lets just leave it at that."* They were playing 'good cop-bad cop' probably from boredom.

In the end, 'good cop' won - and they gave the soldier a ride in the police car back to Knutsford, where he managed to get a lift and continue his journey home.

At home the next day, he was describing the previous nights rather strange encounter, and was intrigued, but not too surprised, when he discovered that the spot on the A50 at Knutsford where he had been waiting, at Mere Corner, was the site of the dumping of the body of Harry Baker, some ten days previously.

The soldier concerned was the author, but who was the mysterious stranger?

Was it a hallucination, a ghoulish spectator, or even a ghostly visitor to the scene, or maybe even the killer?

Well they all seem to be equally unlikely explanations, but the answers to this fifty year old mystery still remain hidden, even to this day.

We can, nevertheless remember the victim, Mr Harry Baker and his family, and pray that he may now be resting in peace.

CHAPTER THIRTEEN

'Going to the Pictures'

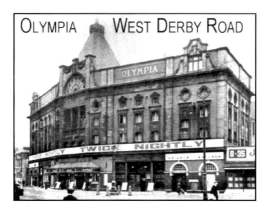

The history of cinema in Liverpool begins in the early years of the 20th century. One of the earliest cinemas, and certainly the largest was the Olympia Theatre (now The Locarno) in West Derby Road.

The Olympia began its life as a variety theatre, and it opened for the first time in 1905.

During its first 20 years, the Olympia featured a variety of diferent types of show, including a Circus, Water Pageant, Opera, Ballet, Classical Music and Pantomimes.

In 1925, it was converted from a variety theatre to a movie theatre with a seating capacity of over 3,500 and featured a 24 piece orchestra to accompany the silent films that it showed.

Four years later, the Olympia became the first in Liverpool to be equipped for the exhibition of sound films.

The first talkie film to be shown there was called The Singing Fool, and starred the singer Al Jolson. In 1948 just after the war, the Olympia was converted into a Ballroom, and renamed the Locarno. This was fifteen years before the arrival of Beatlemania, and for teenagers in Liverpool at that time, the Locarno represented a world of glamour, entertainment and romance. Well it did for me anyway.

Today, the Locarno is thriving once more with a host of diverse events, concerts, comedy, boxing, fashion shows, club nights and more.

However, a night out at the cinema in the golden years of the 1930s, 40s and 50s, for the ordinary member of the public (and we were all quite happy to be ordinary in those days), was the entertainment highlight of the week.

In terms of mass entertainment, there was a choice of staying at home and listening to the radio, with perhaps an occasional visit to the theatre, or to one of the numerous Dance Halls which were dotted around the city. For men, it was usually to one of the even more numerous pubs which were to be found at the corner of most roads, but for the great majority, men women and children, it was going to 'The Pictures'.

There were usually three performances, five days a week except Sunday. The matinee, which usually began about two o'clock and lasted till about 4.30 in the afternoon. The main showing would be the evening performance, which was known as 'the first house'.

This would usually began at perhaps 5.30 in the evening, and the second house, which usually began at 8.00pm.

The average cinema would have had a main entrance which was quite luxurious by the standards of the time, with marble floors in the foyer, and fancy decorations and lots of plush crimson curtains hanging from the walls.

When first entering the local 'Palace of Dreams' you would probably ask for the stalls, or up in the balcony, and then pay at the little kiosk over in the corner.

Everything in those days was about social class. For the lower orders, the young, and those who didn't have the price of a ticket for the main entrance, going to the cinema usually meant queuing along the side entrance, which ran along the building well out of sight of the main entrance.

It would usually involve people standing and queuing, very often in the pouring rain, for seats in one of the first 20 or

30 rows of the stalls, and woe betide anyone who was caught trying to sneak from the pit up to the stalls although of course many of us did.

After people had been queuing out in the rain for some time , and then coming into the warm cinema, some very distinctive odours would start to become noticeable, and fleas or bugs, which were very often present in people's clothes, would become shall we say, even more active. I well remember one of the many strange practices (even for those times) which happened when people were deep in concentration at a particularly absorbing part of the film.

The Atlas Cinema - Rice Lane

A couple of the usherettes, (they were the ladies who took the tickets and showed people to their seats), would quietly walk down the side aisles and spray into the air, a disinfectant mixture, from a pressurised container. This was believed to be DDT, and the vaporised liquid hung like a mist until it gradually settled over the audience, who seemed to be oblivious to the situation.

I have often wondered what its after effects were, no doubt it would have sorted out the fleas and bugs, but its adverse side effects would have been less than beneficial to the unsuspecting audience.

A typical night's entertainment at the cinema would begin with a newsreel and then be followed by a short film, usually a travelogue or something similar.

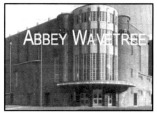

Then came the 'big picture', which was called the feature film, and was usually an American thriller or a gangster film.

Probably the most popular films of all, were the big American musicals like, Oklahoma, South Pacific, or Calamity Jane.

In those days, the end of the film programme was always followed by the national anthem, *'God Save The Queen'*, and believe it or not, everybody would be required to stand to attention whilst it was played, and did so, apart from those who were asleep.

As soon as the national anthem was finished, a rousing military march, usually one of Souza's, would have everyone standing up and marching up the aisle towards the exit in double quick time (some of them still half asleep).

It was then time for the audience to leave their dreams behind, and return to the humdrum reality of those times.

People in those days, before the arrival of television for the masses, days which were unbelievably drab when compared with today's enormous choices in mass entertainment, were very dependent on the escapism that 'going to the pictures' provided for them. Towards the end of the 1940s, the Rank Organisation, founded in 1937 by Flour Milling tycoon, J. Arthur Rank, became the dominant force behind British film-making.

Among the most significant films produced during this period were Brief Encounter (1945), and the Dickens adaptations - Great Expectations (1946) and Oliver Twist (1948), Carol Reed's thrillers Odd Man Out (1947) and The Third Man (1949).

These films helped to make stars of actors like John Mills, Jack Hawkins and Kenneth More, and some of the most successful of them included The Cruel Sea (1953), The Dam Busters (1954), The Colditz Story (1955) and Reach for the Sky (1956).

Popular J Arthur Rank comedy series included the St Trinians films and the "Doctor" series, beginning with Doctor in the House in 1954, and other notable comedy successes, such as Genevieve in 1953.

After a string of successful films, Ealing Studios finally ceased production in 1958, and the studios were taken over by the BBC for television production.

Films with a British dimension have had, and are still having, enormous worldwide commercial success. The top seven highest-grossing films of all time have some British historical, cultural or creative dimensions: The Titanic, Lord of the Rings, Pirates of the Caribbean and the Harry Potter movies. Although the golden age of cinema has died of natural causes, to many people of the older generation it still holds a special place in their heart. Along with the dance halls, these were places were boy would meet girl and go to the pictures on their first date, where perhaps romance might blossom, and in some cases, would eventually lead to marriage.

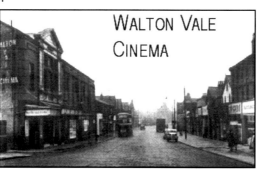

It's no wonder that the cinema eventually became known as the 'Palace of Dreams'.

Entrance to the Palace of Dreams

CHAPTER FOURTEEN

The Ferrari Racing Team in Walton

Rice Lane Garage - 1929

The Car Sales showroom located in Rice Lane Walton, and which was formerly known as the Rice Lane Garage, was built in the 1920s as a small workshop and petrol station. The location was picked by Ferrari's Grand Prix Racing Team in 1955 to be their workshop base for their Formula One racing cars.

The Ferrari team was competing in the British Grand Prix of 1955, which was to be held at the Aintree car racing circuit.

The Ferrari team of mechanics had decided to use the workshops of this small suburban garage as a base to prepare their racing cars for the big event.

It was considered a great honour for the garage to be chosen by Ferrari as their race headquarters, and caused considerable excitement in the local area.

Situated alongside the famous Aintree racecourse, home of the Grand National horse race, the Aintree car racing track was first used in 1954. It was three miles in length and very fast.

As a result it quickly rose to prominence in the austerity of post-war Britain. and Aintree was picked to host the British Grand Prix in 1955 - this turned out to be a memorable race as Stirling Moss took on and beat his Mercedes-Benz team mate Juan-Manuel Fangio.

Aintree Grand Prix

The British Grand Prix became the sixth round of the World Championship.

The race had always been held at Silverstone, but for the 1955 season the Royal Automobile Club decided that the race

would be held at the Aintree racecourse in the outskirts of Liverpool. From 1955 until 1964 the venue staged four British and one European Grand Prix with the best drivers in the world competing around its circuit. Stirling Moss made history there in 1957 by being the first British driver to win a Grand Prix in a British car.   The 'Vanwall' carried him to victory with a little help from his team mate Tony Brooks, who handed over his car when Moss's own car hit trouble. As well as the Grand Prix, many other international races took place at Aintree during this period.

In the 1955 Grand Prix, the Mercedes-Benz team was the favourite for success but the Maserati 250Fs were competitive even if Ferrari was struggling. Vanwall, Gordini, Connaught and Cooper (with Jack Brabham making his World Championship debut) were all represented, but Mercedes-Benz was dominant with Stirling Moss fastest by two-tenths from his team mate Juan-Manuel Fangio.

Moss took the lead at the start, but Fangio quickly moved ahead only to see Moss win back the position on the third lap- Fangio leading for a few laps, and then Moss surging ahead again.

The two continued to lap nose-to-tail for the rest of the afternoon, but at the finish it was Moss who took the flag first - to the delight of the huge Aintree crowd.

It has often been said that Fangio allowed Moss to win, but Fangio never admitted to it. Behind them, Behra had started poorly and the two Mercedes of Kling and Taruffi had passed him. These two were separated when Taruffi dropped behind the second Maserati, being driven by Roberto Mieres. When Behra dropped out on the tenth lap with a broken oil pipe, Mieres was left as the leading Maserati.

By this time, up ahead, Fangio had retaken the lead. Then, to a great roar from the crowd, Moss surged past him.

The two of them continued nose to tail for lap after lap of the 270-mile race, during the course of which Moss set a new lap record of 89 miles an hour.

In the end, by the merest of whiskers, translated by the clock-watchers into just two-tenths of a second, Moss took the chequered flag. Behind them, completing a perfect finish, were the other two Mercedes, with Kling third and Taruffi fourth.

Luigi Musso in a Maserati was fifth, and a Ferrari was sixth. This was driven mostly by Britain's Mike Hawthorn, but he eventually succumbed to sunstroke, not exactly commonplace in sports events held in Liverpool, and his seat was taken by a Ferrari team-mate. Hawthorn was not the only one to suffer in the heat.

There were 15 entrants who retired and in the end, after 90 laps, only nine of the 24 starters finished the race.

This was the first grand prix held at Aintree, and it was generally agreed to be a resounding success.

For ten years Liverpool hosted the best international races of the period with star names and teams visiting the city.

Mercedes, Jaguar, and Ferrari teams raced here, with drivers like Moss, Hawthorn, Fangio, Clark and Hill competing in an era when Britain ruled the sport.

It shared the grandstands with the racecourse, and its facilities were no doubt part of the reason why a splendid crowd of 120,000 was attracted to the grand prix, the largest crowd ever to attend a motoring event in Britain.

Aintree continued as a club race circuit into the 1980's using a loop to take the cars away from the main complex, and still hosts car sprints and motorcycle races. The fifty year anniversary of when cars first used the full circuit, was held in November 2004.

The motor racing circuit ran alongside the main stands and enclosures before following the layout of the horse racing course out towards Bechers Brook.

Today Aintree is the home of Liverpool Motor Club which has possibly the longest history of any motor club in the UK, dating back over 110 years to 1896.

You can follow in the tracks of Fangio, Brooks & Moss, and drive the famous Aintree Circuit. where Stirling Moss secured his first ever Grand Prix win!

The Aintree Circuit also plays host to the Aintree Motorcycle Racing Club which stages various motorcycle racing events at Aintree throughout the year.

CHAPTER FIFTEEN

How Mr Hartley Outwitted Mr Hitler

During the Second World War, on the site which is now occupied by the playing fields of Archbishop Beck School, there was a huge trench, twenty feet wide and ten feet deep, which ran across the field from Cedar Road to Long Lane.

It was said at the time that it was a 'tank trap' (most unlikely). It was more likely a decoy to confuse German Bombers, as it ran parallel to the railway cutting alongside the field, thus making it more difficult for German bombers to distinguish from the air the 'tank traps' from the actual railway cutting.

This trench, which was about the width and depth of the adjacent railway cutting, and ran parallel to the empty field, soon became known locally as the 'tank traps'.

The tank traps were very popular with local children as a playing area, as they easily lent themselves, with a bit of imagination, as the setting for jungle warfare, mediaeval battlefields, and Wild West canyons during local children's games.

Whether Mr Hartley's deception worked or not, we cannot be sure, but it may well have done so, as the factory and its surroundings, managed to survive the war intact. Ironically, towards the end of the war, German prisoners of war were brought to the site from

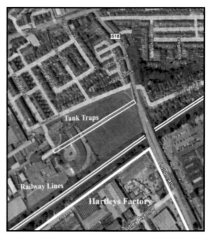

the prisoner of war camp at Huyton and made to fill in the huge crater.

During the Second World War, many important large industrial buildings were camouflaged with green and brown paint, and one of these was Hartley's Jam factory at Aintree.

As the factory was situated right alongside an important railway line, the owners decided on a plan of action to try to fool the German bombers.

They are reputed to have painted the flat roof of the Hartley's factory green, so that from the air it would resemble a large field.

One of the urban myths associated with that time and place, was that they also placed on the factory roof a number of dummy cattle, to increase the illusion that the site was actually a field.

This idea was abandoned after high winds blew the dummy cattle off the roof and spread them around the vicinity of the factory.

It would seem an absurdity to relate such a story today, but during the war the fact that an idea was absurd did not automatically exclude it from being used in the war effort.

Some of the most bizarre ideas were employed to great effect. I well remember being told a wartime story about cars being filled up with coal gas as a fuel,which was supplied from the local gas works. I was quite sure at the time that this was a windup, and when the gentleman described the cars as having a six-foot diameter rubber tank on its roof, I felt he had gone a bit too far.

So I placed a bet of five pounds with him and unfortunately for me he brought in to work the next day a picture of the said gas powered car. Doh.

During the Second World War, and more particularly during the bombing raids which were devastating large parts of Liverpool, it was decided that some attempt would be made to hinder the German bombers in their attempts to destroy the city.

A number of different means were employed to try to achieve this. The most effective means would obviously have been to have fighter aircraft on patrol, in order to intercept and destroy the bombers.

Although Liverpool was strategically, one of the most important areas in the country at that time, because of its docks and its role in supplying the country with much needed food and war equipment. However, fighter aircraft to perform these duties were in dangerously short supply.

A small number of fighter aircraft bases were situated around the Merseyside area, one of these was at Hooton, on the site of what is now the Vauxhall car factory, and another at Sealand on the site of what is now the British Aerospace factory, but in real terms Liverpool was almost defenceless in the first twelve months of the war, and was very much at the mercy of the waves of German bombers, which came at night across the North Sea.

Other means had to be found to deter the bombers, even if they were unable to prevent them altogether.

One of the methods employed as a deterrent, was the use of gas filled dirigibles in various locations across the area.

Their popular name was Barrage Balloons, and they were anchored by cables to the ground in order to control their height, and to prevent them from drifting away.

The general idea was that low-flying bombers would crash into the balloons and ignite them, thereby destroying the plane.

I would very much doubt their effectiveness, but like so many of the measures adopted at the beginning of the war, their additional purpose would be to reassure the population that they were being protected, and were not completely at the mercy of the enemy.

Returning to the subject of the many bizarre ideas which popped up during the Second World War, the image shown on the previous page is of a German bomber flying alongside aerial barrage balloons. Take a look at the weird cutting contraption which is fastened to the front of the wings, this was designed to sever the cables anchoring the balloon to the ground and allowing the bombers access to their targets

Another more effective method of protection against the bombers, was the blackout.

This involved almost all artificial light, as well as all street lighting, being extinguished at night, and vehicles headlamps were fitted with shutters which directed the light beam downwards, and effectively eliminated the glare of headlights.

To complete the 'blackout' windows in all buildings were either fitted with black curtain material or in many cases, painted black all over.

Looking back now, after over 50 years, it is clear that in

numerous ways the war had brought about major changes to many everyday situations, both big and small, and after the war had ended, it took quite a number of years before all the countless traces of those strange war time events had disappeared.

CHAPTER SIXTEEN

Walton's Unholy Trinity

Walton Hospital was the birthplace of the author in March 1937, its other claim to fame came a bit later in 1942, as it was also the birthplace of Paul McCartney.

The Victorian institution originally known as the Walton Workhouse, became a hospital in 1922, with a large and a very busy maternity section, and it was in this hospital on the 18 June 1942, that Paul McCartney was first introduced to the world.

Paul's mother was a nurse in the maternity ward of the hospital and so mother and baby would probably be quite well looked after by her other nursing colleagues.

Paul McCartney, is listed in the Guinness Book of Records as the most successful musician and composer in popular music history with sales of 100 million singles and 60 gold discs. He has achieved twenty-nine number-one singles in the U.S., twenty of them with The Beatles, the rest with Wings and as a solo artist.

Perhaps enough has been written already about Mr McCartney, some might say more than enough.

The Hospital at Walton was originally known as The Walton Workhouse, and was built by the West Derby Union to supplement the already overcrowded Mill Road Workhouse. Opened on April 15th 1868, at a cost of £70,000, it comprised of 33 acres of land with a building of 600-foot frontage, and 'accommodation' for 1600 paupers.

English law assumed that the poor would accept such work and relief as the parish provided.

It was expected that the offer of work in their own homes would not be felt as harsh and punitive by the poor. One of the aims of the Poor Law was to prevent those who were poor, from becoming detached from their place of origin, and so to discourage them from vagrancy. They set up 'Houses of Correction' in each county where work was carried out by the unemployed at the local rates of pay, and also where work could be enforced on the idle and those labelled as vagabonds. But the element of punishment soon became stronger, and the houses, the workhouses that it is, became an early form of jail, quite separate from the parish workhouse.   The law made various distinctions between those it considered 'deserving' and those it decided were the 'undeserving' poor.

Prior to the passing of The Poor Law, it had previously been considered a Christian duty to carry out the instructions laid down in the gospel -

To feed the hungry, give drink to the thirsty, welcome the stranger, clothe the naked, visit the sick, visit the prisoner, and to bury the dead.

After the Reformation, many of these values disappeared and the poor were left without help. It became increasingly clear that something had to be done to help those who were genuinely in need, and something else had to be done about the increasing numbers of those who chose to beg and steal, rather than work.

In 1552, Parish registers of poor were introduced. This meant that there was now an official register of the poor in each parish.

Categories were also drawn up for different types of poverty, and for beggars that were found on the streets.

The Deserving Poor   This category was for those people who wanted to work but were unable to find suitable employment. These people were to be given help in the form of clothes, food or maybe money (Outdoor Relief), and those who were too old, young or ill to work.

These people were to be looked after in almshouses,

orphanages, workhouses or hospitals. Orphans and children of the poor were to be given an apprenticeship to a tradesman.

The Undeserving Poor Also called idle beggars, (they still are), or sturdy beggars, this category was for those who could work, but chose not to.

They were to be whipped through the town until they learnt the error of their ways. In 1572 it was made compulsory that all people pay a local poor tax. The funds raised were to help the deserving poor. It was made law that every district would have an Overseer of the Poor. The overseer had to do the following things:

1. Work out how much money would be needed for the numbers of poor in that district and set the poor rate accordingly.   2. Collect the poor rate from property owners. 3. Relieve the poor by dispensing either food or money, and supervising the parish poor house.

In 1601 an act of Parliament called The Poor Law was passed by Parliament. This act brought together all the measures listed above into one legal document. It was designed to ensure that workhouses were unpleasant places, and paupers would be subjected to numerous petty indignities, a place where only the truly desperate would apply. Families would be split up, given food that was bland and insufficient, and forced to carry out hard and monotonous work.

A public enquiry into the conditions which existed at the Huddersfield workhouse in 1841 stated *'they are forced to the conclusion that the sick and poor have been most shamefully neglected; that they have been and still are, devoid of the necessary articles of clothing and bedding; that they have been suffered to remain for weeks at a time in the most filthy and disgusting state; that patients have been allowed to remain for nine weeks together without change of linen or of bed clothing: that beds in which patients suffering typhus have died in one after another, have been again and again and repeatedly used for fresh patients without any change or attempt at purification; that the said beds were only bags of straw and shavings, for the most part laid on the floor, and that the whole swarmed with lice; that two patients suffering in infectious fever, were almost constantly put together in one bed; that it not infrequently happened that one would be ragingly delirious, when the other was dying; and that it is a fact that a living patient has occupied the same bed with a corpse for a considerable period after death; and that the patients have been for months together without properly appointed nurses to attend to them'.*

The workhouse at Walton formed part of a trinity of institutions, established during the 19th century by the Victorian establishment to accommodate the 'great unwashed' of Liverpool. The Workhouse, Walton Prison, and eventually Walton Park Cemetery.

Life for the pauper community consisted of just the most basic provisions and very strict discipline. Walton Workhouse, the name by which it became later known, had it's own burial ground within the confines of the site, and then finally, could not accept any more graves after 20,000 paupers had been interred, and so it was closed.

In future, pauper burials would be at Walton Park Cemetery just a quarter of a mile further along Rice Lane. In 1913 the name Walton Workhouse was changed to The Walton Poor Law Institution, and then to The Walton Infirmary. From 1913, the care of the paupers fell into the hands of a great humanitarian: Dr. Henry McWilliams, and then conditions were greatly improved. Then finally in 1922, it became known as Walton Hospital, and by 1940, only seven poor law inmates remained. Probably the most striking (if you will kindly pardon the pun) feature of the hospital is the clock tower, which was largely built by the paupers themselves.

One the many callous and inhuman aspects of the workhouse system was the fact that children were not allowed to be with their parents.

Once their parents had entered the workhouse, the youngsters would then be transferred to one of the specially built children's homes in the area, such as The Cottage Homes, or the Kirkdale Industrial School.

After March 1930, the West Derby Union ceased to exist, and the Poor Law administrative functions belonging to the Board of Guardians were separated and transferred respectively to the Liverpool City Council, Bootle County Borough Council and Lancashire County Council.

In Liverpool a Public Assistance Committee was appointed consisting of members of Liverpool City Council, and the remainder were representatives of various Public Authorities and local voluntary organisations.

The newly formed Public Assistance Committee became

responsible for the following institutions which later became hospitals: Alder Hey Hospital, Belmont Road Institution, Mill Road Infirmary, Smithdown Road Hospital and Walton Hospital. The National Assistance Act 1948 and National Health Service Act 1946 came into effect from 5 July 1948 and brought an end to the Poor Law.

Walton Prison

Walton was Liverpool's second major prison and was built between 1850 and 1854 and constructed in Hornby Road, Liverpool with an initial capacity for 1,000 inmates.

It was designed to take both male and female prisoners who had been sentenced at the Liverpool Assizes, and was one of the largest and most modern prisons in England in its day.

The image shown here is of Walton in its present form, with the 19th century tower still visible above the modern additions to the buildings.

Walton Prison Liverpool

Walton Prison, has had a long and sometimes infamous career. It was purpose built to replace it's even more infamous predecessor, which had been located in Kirkdale.

When the new prison had been completed, those prisoners who were to be relocated from Kirkdale to Walton were chained together and marched in small batches between the old establishment in Kirkdale, and the new modern prison at Walton. It must have made quite a strange and rather sad spectacle.

After the closure of Kirkdale Gaol, the new prison at Walton became the place of execution for those prisoners who had been sentenced to death at the Crown Court.

From 1892, the gallows remained at Walton, and later a standard execution facility was constructed at the prison within one of the wings containing a permanent gallows, which was to remain in use until 1964.

Between 1887 and 1964, 60 men and 2 women were hung in Walton jail.

Many strange and unusual events were connected to those who were to be guests of HM Prison at Walton.

Of these, one of the most bizarre cases concerned three foreign seamen accused of mutiny and murder on the high seas, while serving aboard a British registered vessel, the three-masted barque Veronica, out of St. John, New Brunswick.

This extraordinary case opened at Liverpool's St George's Hall on the 12th of May 1903.

The Crown prosecution was conducted by Mr Frederick Edwin Smith, (Lord Birkenhead), who coincidentally, was also the Conservative MP for Walton, and a prominent QC of the early 20th century.

He is perhaps best remembered today, if at all, as Winston Churchill's great personal and political friend until Smith's untimely death at age 58.

The three accused seamen were Gustav Rau, and Otto Monson (both German) and Willem Schmidt (Dutch) who were accused of killing Alexander Shaw, the British captain of the ship *Veronica*, and six members of his crew.

The murders were alleged to have taken place aboard the vessel in December 1902, on a voyage from the American port of Gulfport, Louisiana to Montevideo in Uruguay, at sea off the coast of South America.

They were only tried on the single charge of murdering the captain, the other charges being held in reserve, in the unlikely event that they were acquitted of this one.

While at sea, the German crewmen of the *Veronica* became upset with their British shipmates and while off the northeast coast of Brazil, they murdered Captain Shaw and the crew, and set the ship on fire.

In December 1902, the mutineers landed on the small island of Tuotoia which forms a part of the bar at the mouth of the Rio Parnaiba in northeastern Brazil.

The killings came to light when the five men (Rau, Monson, Schmidt, Henry Flohr and Moses Thomas were picked up by a British freighter, the SS *Brunswick*, off the coast of Brazil.) They told their rescuers an incredible story. According to the German

SS Veronica.

seamen, the *Veronica* had started its voyage to Montevideo with a crew of 12 men, of whom two had died in accidents at sea. They then had a fire on board, and had abandoned ship in one of the ship's two life boats, losing contact with the remaining members of the crew in the second boat. One of the five rescued men, Moses Thomas, seemed afraid of the others and asked to be kept separate from them.

It was also noticed that Gustav Rau had some of the captain's clothing on, which seemed odd to the *Brunswick*'s captain.

The *Brunswick* made its way home to England arriving at Liverpool in December 1903. Moses Thomas told its captain that the missing crew of the *Veronica* had really been murdered by the other 4 survivors, although they vehemently denied this, and stuck to the story of the fire, accusing Thomas of inciting the mutiny and killing the rest of the crew.

The Captain of the *Brunswick* was deeply suspicious of the men's story and handed all five over to the police when he docked in Liverpool. Henry Flohr decided to change his story and support Thomas' version of events.

Moses Thomas related to the police at Liverpool what had really happened on the SS *Veronica* off the coast of South America. The first mate, Alexander McLeod, was the first to be murdered by Schmidt and Rau, who had quarrelled with him over his authoritarian management style. McLeod was battered to death and thrown overboard. Once they had murdered First Mate McLeod, they were then at serious risk, so it was decided to kill any other member of the crew who would not join them.

Then four other crewmen were battered and thrown into the sea, while Captain Shaw and another man were shot prior to being thrown overboard.

The final crewman jumped over the side and was shot dead in the water.

The German seamen made a fatal mistake however by bringing the ship's cook Moses Thomas, an American Negro with them.

On the long voyage to England, Moses Thomas related the tale of horror aboard the *Veronica* to the ship's master, Captain Browne.

After the *Brunswick* reached Liverpool in late January, three of the alleged murderers were arrested and held at Walton Prison until the trial which commenced on May 12, 1903, at the Liverpool Assizes.

Since the ship's pilot, Captain Antoine Bellande was the last person to see the crew of the *Veronica* alive, when he piloted the vessel out of Gulfport in Louisiana, he was called to travel from the USA to England to testify at the trial in Liverpool.

The trial was to last 3 days before Mr. Justice Lawrence, and on the 14th of May, all three defendants were found guilty and were sentenced to death by hanging.

Inspector Duckworth

Moses Thomas   Antoine Bellande   Sgt. Ford,

The fourth seaman, Otto Monsson, was reprieved following the jury's recommendation to mercy, and also because of his age, but the two older men, Rau and Schmidt, were taken from the court to the condemned cells at Walton Prison to await their grisly fate - death by hanging. Just 3 weeks later, at 8.00 a.m. on the morning of Tuesday, the 2nd of June 1903, they were brought together again for the final time, this time side by side on the gallows, and hanged by William Billington, assisted by John Billington.

This was the first of a number of double executions at Walton. Ten years later an African American seaman named Young Hill was working on a cargo ship the SS Antillian, looking after the mules (a muleteer as his position was known).

The SS Antillian had sailed from America to Avonmouth Docks at Bristol, and was then making its way to Liverpool, when on the night of the 26th of July in 1915, Hill cut the throat of fellow crew member, James Crawford. Apparently, the motive for the killing was a disagreement of the cleanliness of some water in a bucket. Hill was immediately arrested when the Antillian docked at Liverpool and was tried at Liverpool Assizes at St George's Hall on the 29th of October 1915.

There was only one condemned cell at Walton and this was allocated to Hill. Another condemned prisoner named Thornley was accommodated in the hospital wing prior to being moved to a cell closer to the gallows on the eve of his execution. The prison authorities decided to go for another cost effective, two for the price of one execution. The official hangman at the time, Ellis, made the usual preparations on the Sunday evening, Ellis first pinioned Thornley's hands behind his back, and then Hill, before they were both led to the gallows by two pairs of warders.

Thornley was first on the trapdoors and was immediately hooded and noosed, a sight which completely unnerved Young Hill who began to faint. Ellis was able to release the trap before Hill collapsed and they both plummeted down together. He recorded that this double execution took 82 seconds to complete.

Walton was to achieve its place in the history books of crime and punishment in 1964, when one of the two final executions in Britain took place here on Thursday the 13th of August 1964, when Peter Allen was hanged at Walton, while his co-defendant, Evans (real name John Robson Walby), was hanged at the same moment, at Strangeways Prison in Manchester. Thus ended capital punishment in Britain, and the death penalty was now effectively abolished.

In 2008, some prisoners were serving less than 5 years for offences which would have seen them hang in 1964.

Over recent years a number of small additional prisons have been built in and around the Merseyside area. Having only one Prison (rather like having only one Cathedral) would not really match the requirements, or the aspirations, of a City like Liverpool.

Walton Park Cemetery

A part of the official plan to deal with those who were surplus to the requirements of the emerging industrial society (Charles Dickens 'surplus population' again), was the Pauper's Grave.

This was the system that was in place to accommodate those who died, and were unfortunate enough to be in that category, often having remained there from cradle to the grave. It was not meant to be in any sense, a welfare state as we know it, more a way of maintaining a tidy and well ordered environment for the middle and upper classes.

The institutional facilities that were brought into operation were primarily to punish those who were considered to be poor because of their own laziness, and to further discourage begging and any similar attempts to exist without having made any contribution to their own well being.

Hospitals, or Infirmaries as they were known at that time, existed as institutions for poor people to be treated only on an emergency basis and in a very elementary way.

For those who did not survive the primitive medical treatments available there, an equally rudimentary system of burial was provided, which came to be known as the 'pauper's grave'

Having been labelled as a pauper, you would think that would have been sufficient to ensure that the rigid class system would be adequately served. However, equally as important for maintaining the class structure, was the maintenance of the religious status quo, so the burial places of the 19th century were maintained on a sectarian basis, and at the bottom layer of the social hierarchy were the indeterminate and anonymous graves of those who had died in the workhouse.

Walton Park Cemetery was situated directly opposite to Walton Prison, either by design or by coincidence, and those who were unfortunate enough to die in the prison, had a very short journey across to the other side of Hornby Road, probably the shortest journey of their life There, they would be placed in the same category, and probably in the same section, which took people from the workhouse, and from other similar establishments, and provided them with their last resting place.

The most well known of those whose last resting place was to be in the paupers section of Walton Cemetery, was the nineteenth century author Robert Tressell, internationally known author of a book featuring the elements of socialism which has since become a classic of it's type.

Tressell's novel is about the underclass of Edwardian society, and about exploitative employment when the only safety nets were charity, the workhouse, and the grave. Following the fortunes of a group of painters and decorators, and the attempts to rouse their political will by the Socialist visionary Frank Owen, the book is a highly entertaining story and passionate appeal for a fairer way of life.

On of the most famous passages in the book, and the most quoted, is 'The Great Money Trick'. It was described by him as follows:

"These pieces of bread represent the raw materials which exist naturally in, and on the earth, for the use of mankind; they were not made by any human being, but were created for the benefit and sustenance of all, the same as were the air and the light of the Sun". "Now," continued Owen, "I am a capitalist; or rather I represent the landlord and capitalist class. That is to say, all these raw materials belong to me. "Now you three represent the working class. You have nothing, and although I have these raw materials, they are of no use to me. What I need is the things that can be made out of these raw materials by work. But first I must explain that I possess something else beside the raw materials. These three knives represent all the machinery of production; the factories, tools, railways, and so forth, without which the necessaries of life cannot be produced in abundance. And these three coins" - taking three half pennies from his pocket - "represent my money, capital." I am going to invest all my money in various industries, so as to give you plenty of work. I shall pay each of you one pound per week, and a week's work is that you must each produce three of these square blocks. For doing this work

you will each receive your wages; "These blocks represent the necessaries of life. You can't live without some of these things, but as they belong to me, you will have to buy them from me: my price for these blocks is one pound for each block." As the working classes were in need of the necessaries of life and as they could not eat, drink or wear the useless money, they were compelled to agree to the capitalist's terms.

They each bought back, and at once consumed, one-third of the produce of their labour.

The capitalist class also devoured two of the square blocks, and so the net result of the week's work was that the kind capitalist had consumed two pounds worth of things produced by the labour of others, and reckoning the squares at their market value of one pound each.

He had more than doubled his capital, for he still possessed the three pounds in money and in addition four pounds worth of goods.

As for the working classes, having each consumed the pound's worth of necessaries they had bought with their

wages, they were again in precisely the same condition as when they had started work - they had nothing."

It asks questions that are still being asked today: why do your wages bear no relation to the value of your work?

Why do fat cats get richer when you don't?.

Tressell's answers are "The Great Money Trick" and the "philanthropy" of an unenlightened workforce, who give away their rights and aspirations to a decent life so freely, in return for so little.

Intellectually enlightening, deeply moving and funny, *The Ragged Trousered Philanthropists* is a book that changes lives.

He completed his book, *The Ragged Trousered Philanthropists* in 1910, but initially, the 1,600 page-long hand-written manuscripts were rejected by the three publishing houses that he submitted his work to.

The rejection of his book severely depressed him, and at one point, his daughter had to save the manuscripts, when he tried to burn them out of frustration. The author's actual name was Robert Noonan, but he signed the book as 'Robert Tressell', for fear of reprisals, but he still failed to find a publisher.

He became disillusioned and unhappy with his life in Britain, so that August he set off to Liverpool to make arrangements for emigration to Canada.

In November he became seriously ill and he was admitted to the Liverpool Workhouse Infirmary. On 3 February 1911 a telegram informed his daughter that he had died of 'cardiac failure'.

Kathleen mentioned her father's novel to a friend of hers, writer Jessie Pope, who recommended it to her publisher.

In April 1914, the publisher bought the rights to the book for £25, and it appeared in Britain, Canada and the United States later that year

And so he, like so many others who became victims of

the poverty trap, he was later buried in a mass grave along with twelve other paupers in Walton Cemetery, the grave yard situated opposite to Walton Prison.

The location of the grave was not discovered until 1970, when through the diligent efforts of a local man, the late John Nettleton, the records of his burial and the exact site were finally identified.

The last resting place of Robert Tressell is now marked with a commemorative plaque at the Cemetery, near to the Hornby Road entrance, opposite to Walton Prison.

His novel was described as the first truly imaginative portrayal of life written from a working-class perspective, and a passionate defence of socialist ideals. It was voted 'most influential book' in a survey of Labour MP's in the New Statesman (Interesting). We conclude this trinity of historic Walton institutions, Walton Hospital, Walton Park Cemetery, and Walton Prison, and a glimpse at how things used to be for the less fortunate members of society, the ones who were born in the wrong place and at the wrong time. Time and place was the reason why their experience was so different from ours. We citizens of the twenty first century, who have inherited so much of the social improvements that were fought for and suffered for, and eventually won, by those countless, faceless, generations of people from the past, certainly have very much to thank them for.

CHAPTER SEVENTEEN

Where Did Your Dad work?

Up until the early nineteen eighties, the City of Liverpool was largely inhabited by what is now becoming an almost forgotten species, those who once were proud to be known as 'the working class'.

Previously, large numbers of these hardy and colourful inhabitants had lived and worked there in their natural habitats, which were located all across the city.

Then they gradually began to disappear during the evolution of a new hybrid species, which came to be known as the 'global work force'.

Consequently, the 'working classes' have now evolved into a new, classless and apolitical species, which bears little or no resemblance to those who were once to be found in great numbers, and working at any of these former Liverpool factory locations:

Automatic Telephone and Electric Company - Edge Lane. *Manufacturers of communication equipment.*

Bryant and Mays - Garston. *Safety matches.*

Metal Box - Breeze Hill. Walton, Speke, Aintree. *Metal and cardboard containers.*

Spencers Iron Works - Rice Lane. *Metal fabrications.*

Triumph - Speke. *Car factory.*

Lockheed - Speke. *Aircraft components.*

Dunlop Footwear - Rice Lane. *Wellington boots.*

Barker & Dobsons - Anfield. *Sweets and confectionery.*

Crawfords - Edge Lane. *Biscuits and crackers.*

Reads Tinworks - Bull Lane. *Tin cans.*

English Electric - Dunnings Bridge Road. *Hydro electric turbines.*

Spencers - Bull Lane. *Brick works.*

Royal Ordinance Factory - Long Lane. *Armaments and weapons.*

Taylors - Breeze Hill. *Bakery.*

Hartleys - Long Lane. *Jam and vegetable cannery.*

Napiers - East Lancashire Road. *Electrical switchgear.*

Schweppes. - Aintree. *Mineral water and lemonade.*

Eric Bemrose Ltd. -Long Lane. *Newspaper printers.*

Scotts Ltd - Netherton. *Bakery.*

Harland &Wolfe. - Regent Road. *Ship repair.*

Westinghouse Co - Fazackerley. *Railway signals and brakes.*

Lily Cups Ltd. - Fazackerley. *Drink containers.*

Sayers - Lorenzo Drive. *Bakers and confectioners.*

Tillotsons - Commercial Road. *Containers and printing.*

British American Tobacco - Commercial Road. *Cigarettes and tobacco.*

Meccano - Binns Road. *Dinky and Meccano toys.*

Dunlop Ltd - Speke. *Heavy duty tyre manufacturers.*

Tate & Lyle - Love Lane. *Sugar refinery.*

Ogdens - West Derby Road. *Tobacco.*

Ayrton Saunders - Duke Street. *Pharmaceuticals.*

Mantunna Tea - Wood Street. *Tea blenders.*

Ridgeways - Speke. *Tea blenders.*

British Enka - Aintree. *Synthetic silk and rayons.*

Newforge Foods - *Belle Vale. Manufacturers of Spam canned meat.*

Bibbys - *Food oil refinery*

This is by no means a complete list of the former factories in Liverpool which have been made redundant since the end of world War Two, they only represent the ones which I can remember.   I have not included the enormous amount of people who were employed directly or indirectly in the crewing, servicing, and the repairing of the numerous ships which arrived at, and departed to, the four corners of the world from Liverpool every day.

In a book which is held in Harvard University and written in 1812 by Thomas Kaye entitled 'The Stranger in Liverpool' is a descriptive account of Liverpool and it's environment, the following observations were made of the industries, and the nature of the inhabitants of the town at that time. *'Liverpool though situated in the most extensive manufacturing county in the kingdom is not itself properly speaking a manufacturing town. The vast magnitude of its foreign commerce must necessarily demand the practice of a great number of domestic trades some belonging to shipping in general and others depending on the peculiar nature of the traffic of the port, but it has no kind of manufacture by which it is peculiarly distinguished and which raises it above the level of the rest.*

It has been a matter of enquiry why cotton manufacturing is not carried on to a greater extent [in Liverpool] as the situation is equally convenient for the purchase of raw material and then the exportation of manufactured goods. The internal parts of Lancashire are being supplied with most of the cotton from this port and then returning great quantities of goods to be shipped for foreign orders as a great expense of carriage.

The reason is obvious, that kind of textile business is indigenous to the interior of the county, there business rules, and there it has been matured.

The long established work habits of the people and local circumstances have fixed it there in Manchester, as if always so and it must remain so.

We may add, that great difficulty must attend the establishment of industry of this kind in Liverpool, [at that time, part of the County of Lancashire] where the labouring classes already have sufficient employment [in the maritime industries] of a nature more favourable to their health and independence than those of a cotton factory, where the restrictions of time and confinement for so many hours of the day, enforced with penalties or dismissal.

This kind of occupation is equally as repugnant to the spirit of an English man, as unfavourable to his comforts. There must exist the necessity, which the labouring people here do not feel, and a far greater encouragement must be held out than that trade is paid, and is generally capable of affording, before they could be induced to engage either themselves, or their children, in an employment which imposes customs so foreign to their former habits. Liverpool however has numerous houses for the refining of sugar and extensive pottery factories, iron foundries public breweries etc and the curious stranger will be highly gratified by the visit'

For a variety of reasons, good, bad, and indifferent, these factories became casualties in the struggle by the various vested interests to maximise profit. It was not as if all the products became redundant, far from it. People still drink tea, and eat biscuits, drive cars and fly in planes, and of course, the demand for 'wellies' will be there as long as we have rain.

What has changed is that the supply of labour and services in the UK has now become part of a global market and requires of those who supply them, maximum efficiency and flexibility, at the minimum cost.   Production of basic commodities, and the employment of those who supply them has changed for ever, and for most of those who worked in traditional industries like those former factories listed above, it will never return. One of the most dramatic changes in the world of global economics has been in the manufacturing of consumer goods, with an almost total change of production locations from West to East .

Here is one indication of the way it has happened - the latest trading figures show the China produces 50 % of all the world's shoes, 50% of the worlds cameras, 25% of the world's textiles, 25% of the world's washing machines and a staggering 70% of the world's toys. This profit enhancing re-structuring of nearly all our basic consumer items, is one of the most wasteful and environmentally damaging changes to our economy. Think of the cost, the pollution, and the waste of our dwindling oil supplies, which are involved in shipping just about everything from cars to computers, from shoes to shirts, and just about everything in between over ten thousand nautical miles to reach it's market. Classic, short term benefits producing long term problems.

So there you have it, global economic madness.

CHAPTER EIGHTEEN

Last Orders at the Windsor Castle

During World War Two, the original Windsor Castle Pub on Walton Vale was at the centre of a cluster of buildings, which received a direct hit from an aerial landmine during the May Blitz of 1941.

Needless to say the bombing of the local, was not part of a dastardly German plan to deprive the regulars of their pints of beer. The Windsor Castle pub happened to be in the vicinity of a number of important railway lines leading into the area of Aintree marshalling yards and railway junction. In fact it was less than 100 yards from the main railway line which ran from Liverpool Exchange Station up to Glasgow on the west coast of Scotland. In addition there was also structural damage to Walton RC school, and the complete destruction of a dozen other buildings surrounding the blast area.

One of the after affects of the large aerial bomb which dropped on the Windsor Castle Pub was the formation of a huge crater, which was later brick lined and coated with tar and then converted into a huge emergency water supply tank for the Fire Brigades to use. One of the many problems that arose from the bombings which took place throughout the city during WW2 was the fracturing of the underground water pipes, which then made firefighting almost impossible in many cases. And so the emergency water supply although constructed shortly after the bombing, was never really used for fire fighting afterwards. It did, however, acquire a new use, albeit an unofficial one, as a makeshift open air swimming pool for local young boys.

Although soon after a tragic drowning accident the erection of a barbed wire fence around the walls brought its unofficial swimming pool life to an abrupt end. All over Liverpool at that time there were houses which had been bombed, but in some cases were only partially destroyed, consequently it required a huge operation to enable them to be made safe before being eventually demolished. Ironically, one of the ways this was carried out was by the employment of German prisoners of War, under armed guard, to complete the destruction of the half demolished buildings that had been left by their comrades in the Luftwaffe (German air force). They were based at the large prisoner of war camp at Bluebell Lane in Huyton. Strangely enough, the armed guards were not so much to prevent the prisoners of war from escaping, as for the protection of the Germans POWs against attack from civilians. This would be understandable at that time, as many people had recently lost friends and relatives, either in the bombings on Liverpool, or while serving on the battlefield, in the air, or at sea.

The local contingent of prisoners of war generated a small local industry for the unofficial supply of tobacco which they used for hand rolling cigarettes.

For the civilian population, one of the items which never seem to be in short supply was cigarettes, coinciding with a sizeable demand for tobacco, which was created by the prisoners of war.

And so fortunately, a plentiful supply of tobacco was always available to the small boys of the area from the discarded cigarette ends which were to be found in abundance on almost every street.

Another youthful recycling initiative was horse manure, which was to be found on every main street. This was considered to be a very valuable commodity for fertilising the gardens and allotments, which many families used to grow vegetables in order to supplement their food ration.

Horse-drawn vehicles of every description were still very much in evidence at that time, as were their frequent deposits onto the roads.

I can well remember how strong was the similarity between horse manure, which had been dried, and cigarette tobacco.

It did not take the local boys long to realise the potential for combining the two substances, putting them into a tobacco tin and selling them to the Germans. I doubt whether the recycling aspect of the enterprise was as prominent in the minds of us small boys as was the thought of taking some small revenge against the enemy.

Of course, the prisoners of war did not have any money, and so a system of swapping tobacco in exchange for military insignia, tunic buttons and cap badges formed the basis of the currency which was used for bartering.

Working-class children in those days would seldom, if ever, receive pocket money from their parents, however certain items would be used as the currency of bartering [swops]. Those lucky enough to have uncles or fathers who were seamen travelling between Liverpool and the United States, and who sometimes brought home American comic books, became the aristocracy of the schoolboy bartering system.

It was in fact the scarcity value of these items, the military insignia, badges, and American comic books, which enabled the lucky few who had them, to trade and obtain various other bits of stuff, without having access to money.

I suppose it would be just economics, in its basic form, and not a whole lot different from the macro economics which facilitate trading on a global scale. When carrying out research for a book such as this, it sometimes comes to your attention how many stories lie within other stories. One such story came from an elderly gentleman who had spotted a local story about the Blitz in Liverpool on a BBC web site. This gentleman, having read an account of the Walton Vale bombings, sent me the following personal account of the bombing incident.

'I just spotted the image of the bombing in Walton Vale on the Internet, I was one of the bodies buried there. It was about midnight, and we had been putting out fires in a house in Chevin Road, just off Chapel Avenue, and outside someone shouted "fire bombs in Chapel Avenue." I reckon I was only about 40 ft. away from the explosion - I think it hit the Bank. I saw the spark of ignition and an almighty crack blew me back into Chevin Road and under the two houses that collapsed.

I 'came too' later, as deaf as a door nail. I then saw people being taken past me with their wounds tied up.

I eventually dug myself out and headed into the shelter opposite where people talked at me, but I could not hear anything.

I then headed down Chapel Avenue again, and nearly fell down the sewer.

My sister took me into the air raid shelter shouting, "where is our Harry", I never thought about him (must of lost it a little), anyway Harry came in on a stretcher about an hour later, and cousin Jack did not appear till next morning, and he never knew where he had been'.

Among the buildings destroyed, in addition to the pub, were the shops opposite the pub, the United Reform Church on the corner of Orrell Lane, the Funeral Parlour (where the pub car park is now) and Blessed Sacrament Church, which had its roof blown off. It wasn't all completely rebuilt until the early fifties.

The original Windsor Castle was built around 1902. This would be an important and well used facility during this period, as it is situated on the A59 trunk road and travellers by road northwards to Scotland and beyond, would pass the hotel daily.

The tram shown below would be going either to Fazakerley, or to the tramcar terminus at Aintree. This type of tram was still in use along Walton Vale until the late fifties, when the tram system was made redundant and all the tracks were taken up .

Today, in the twenty-first century, they are now re-inventing tramways as a more environmental solution to traffic pollution and congestion, bet they wish they had left well alone.

The idea that prompted my initial local history project was entitled, *'North Liverpool - Now and Then'* and with it came the realization that many seemingly uneventful locations have a hidden history, which lies just below the surface, and which can at first sight appear to be rather unbelievable.

This is where the ability to illustrate events from the past with images and photographs, can help to tell the story more convincingly.

In researching the material used in this book, I have realised that the last one hundred years have been the most eventful in the overall history of the area.

We have seen many millions of people constantly travelling through Liverpool, both coming and going, two world wars which have brought vast numbers of people to the area, and probably the biggest changes, and the most spectacular events.

Now, at the beginning of the twenty first century, the city is undergoing even more spectacular and far reaching changes, and who knows what effects these will have on the future.

Somehow, without having the historians benefit of hindsight, I rather doubt they will match the dramatic and spectacular events of our more recent past.

CHAPTER NINETEEN

The Very Strange Tale of Alois and Adolf Schicklgruber

Regarding the story of Hitler's visit to Liverpool - did he, or did he not, visit Liverpool in 1911?

My first recollection of hearing about the story of Hitler's so-called visit to Liverpool was at the former ice rink, which was situated in Prescot Road Liverpool.

In the foyer of the ice rink, there was a glass cabinet with various displays in it, and one of them displayed what was purported to be his black ice skating boots, and a little notice by the boots which stated that they were Adolf Hitler's skating boots.

I never paid much attention to that story at the time because it seemed far too unlikely to be true.

Some 20 years later, a lady in the office where I worked in Liverpool, who was the daily cleaner, told me a similar story which I also found a little difficult to believe at first. It concerned a man with the unlikely name of Alois Schicklgruber, an Austrian, and who was without any doubt Hitler's brother, possibly his half brother, but certainly a brother.

She told me that around the area of Grafton Street the story of Hitler's brother living in Stanhope Street was very well remembered by local people.

There is no doubt now that Alois Hitler lived for a period of time in Liverpool. It is also known that he opened a restaurant in Dale Street, which he ran for some years prior to 1911.

He was somewhat erratic in his employment history, and had a number of different jobs in the city. It is also a known fact that he was married to an Irish woman named Brigid Dowling, whom he had met in Dublin, where he was working in one of the big hotels and presumably where she also worked, and they both eventually married and moved over to Liverpool. They then lived in a house in 102 Upper Stanhope Street, off Grafton Street in the south end of the city. That much is true.

The story I heard, was that Hitler had visited his brother in the autumn of 1912, and was reputed to have attended the baptism of the couple's child, who was christened at the church of St Patrick in Park Place.

I enquired of the priest in charge of St Patrick's, if the event did in fact happen, and he said quite emphatically yes, and that it was in the baptismal register of that year. However, Hitler's signature as the godfather of the child Patrick Hitler was not to be seen in the baptismal register.

There has always been doubt about the fact that he had ever visited the city, although Alois's wife, Brigid, wrote a book about the events in the late 1930s, and in it she was quite adamant about Hitler's visit to his brother and sister in law and their son, Patrick.

As there is no clear evidence, other than the testament of Brigid, obviously that would be very difficult to prove.

There is an American book, entitled *'The Life and Death of Adolf Hitler'* written by Robert Payne, and in the book, Brigid is quoted on dates when he arrived in Liverpool, and clearly states the times and places and dates of his visit, which she claims was from about November 1912 till the following April.

Not too many people would wish to substantiate the evidence that they had a visit from Adolf Hitler; as it's not something which most people would see as beneficial.

I am certain, however, that the circumstantial and documentary evidence is very clear that Hitler's brother/half brother Alois Schicklgruber did in fact live in Stanhope Street at the time, that he married Bridget Dowling, and that they produced a son called Patrick Hitler, who was baptised at Saint Patrick's church in Park Place.

In 1914, Alois deserted Brigid and their young son in Liverpool and soon after, he went back to live in Austria.

Brigid and her son William Patrick moved to London in 1924, and lived there till just before the Second World War, when they moved countries and emigrated to America, where eventually Patrick Hitler actually served in the United States Navy. There is no real doubt that much is historically true.

The story begins with William Patrick's father, Alois - Adolf Hitler's older half-brother. He was touring Britain studying, he said, the hotel industry and met a farm girl called Brigid Downey in Dublin in 1909. The couple eloped to London before moving up to Liverpool where Brigid gave birth to their only son, William Patrick, in a flat at 102 Upper Stanhope Street, Toxteth, in 1911.

Alois ran in turn a small restaurant in Dale Street, then a boarding house on Parliament Street and finally a hotel on Mount Pleasant, which went bust. After he became bankrupt, Alois left his wife and young child to fend for themselves and returned to Germany.

When William Patrick grew up he moved to London but by this time his uncle had risen to power in Germany.

For the first, but not last time, the curse of his surname struck and he was laid off from the job he had found. He decided, therefore, to travel to Germany and make full use of the Hitler family connections.

His father and uncle helped him find work there, but the young William Patrick thought that he deserved something better than the book-keeping jobs he was given.

He eventually fell foul of his uncle, when he suggested that if he wasn't found something more befitting a member of the Fuehrer's family, he would go public with rumours that the Nazi leader's grandfather was an Austrian Jew.

This prompted an ultimatum by Hitler: William Patrick was ordered to renounce his British citizenship and take a senior position in the Third Reich. The young man instead chose to flee from Germany.

It was now 1939 and he received a cold welcome in London, so he left England with his mother for a lecture tour of America on the subject of "My Uncle Adolf".

He arrived in New York at the end of March 1939 and

"divested himself of a lot of uncomplimentary remarks about uncle Adolf", according to a report in the *New York Daily News*.

His lectures attracted considerable attention at first but once America was forced into the war at the end of 1941 interest began to wane.

In 1942 William Patrick wrote to President Roosevelt asking to be allowed to join the US Navy. *"I have attempted to join the British forces,"* he wrote. *"The British are an insular people and while they are kind and courteous, it is my impression, rightly or wrongly, that they could not in the long run feel overly cordial or sympathetic towards an individual bearing the name that I have."*

He continued by saying that he and his mother owed a *"great debt"* to the United States and pleaded: *"More than anything else I would like to see active combat as soon as possible and thereby be accepted by my friends and comrades as one of them in this great struggle for liberty."*

As a result of the letter, William Patrick was investigated by the FBI, who found no evidence of any subversive activities, and he was given hope that he may be allowed to join up.

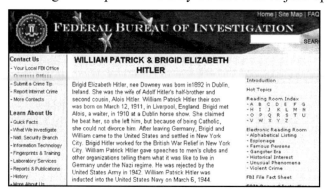

But it wasn't until 1944 that he was finally enlisted into the US navy.

There was one moment of comic coincidence when William Patrick arrived at the draft office and was asked his name by the recruiting officer. "Hitler," he replied. "Glad to see you Hitler," said the officer, "my name's Hess." The event was recorded by several newspapers - it was the last time that William Patrick Hitler was seen or heard of in public. Once in uniform he disappeared from public sight for ever. After the war, inquiries eventually led to a small cemetery beside a freeway in Long Island, where it was found that Brigid and William Patrick shared the same grave. He had died in 1987, 18 years after his mother Brigid.

William Patrick Hitler had first met his wife Phyllis in Germany in the 1930s through her brother.

With war looming, the brother had asked William Patrick to look after his sister Phyllis in New York and dispatched the girl - who was 12 years younger than Patrick Hitler - into his safekeeping. Romance blossomed and the couple married after the war in 1947.

Their three surviving sons - Alex, 52, Louis, 50, and Brian, 36 - fiercely guard their privacy and their family secret. Whether or not Hitler ever lived here in Liverpool is another matter altogether, and is considered extremely unlikely (Thank Goodness).

During the final bombing blitz on Liverpool in the Second World War, the last batch of bombs on Liverpool, were dropped on Upper Stanhope Street, and on the Park Lane area.

The bombs completely destroyed the house in Stanhope Street were Hitler's brother had formerly lived.

Now that's something so bizarre, that you couldn't even make it up.

CHAPTER TWENTY

Aintree Iron - Thank U Very Much

Warbreck Moor - 1890

In the late 19th century, Aintree became an important element of the newly established railway systems which were suddenly springing up everywhere   In the area behind the houses in the left of the picture, there were a large number of railway sidings, and what were known as sheds, where large steam locomotives would be serviced and maintained.

Alongside the Aintree sheds was a huge marshalling yard, called the Aintree grid, and which consisted of many miles of tracks. As well as being called the Aintree grid, it was sometimes known as the 'Aintree Iron'.

At the entrance to the shed was a massive rotating turntable, the 'Aintree Iron', which was used to rotate the heavy steam locomotives and re-direct them into the appropriate shed for maintenance.

The term 'Aintree Iron' was the subject of a pop music hit *'Thank U Very Much'* recorded by the Liverpool group 'The Scaffold' and in 1967 it reached number four in the music charts.

The operation of the sheds, and of the marshalling yards, involved drivers and firemen from all over the country arriving at Aintree throughout the day and night.

The railway company built a huge hostel for their travelling staff, which was formerly situated on the corner of Greenwich Road and Melling Road.

This was a large four storey building, which provided meals and accommodation for hundreds of men at a time. However this was eventually demolished during the late 1960s, and replaced with a private housing estate.

A huge shunting, siding, and maintenance shed would marshall and sort hundreds of freight wagons, while the steam locos would be repaired and serviced inside the Shed. Aintree had a very thriving steam railway facility dating from the late nineteenth century right up to 1967, which was the signal (forgive the pun) for the demise of the steam locomotive in Britain.

On the other side of the Aintree racecourse lies another former railway operations centre at Fazakerley where the expansion of Victorian rail traffic, especially freight, led to the building of the Fazakerley sidings in 1886. Two factories, the Railway Signal Company and the Lancashire and Yorkshire Carriage and Wagon Works were built to manufacture equipment specially for the railways and were operational in the area by 1890. This company produced standard designs of signalling equipment, including signal boxes, which were subsequently adopted by the L&YR itself when it set up its own signalling department at Horwich Works in 1886.

During the period between 1881 and 1891, a number of houses were built to accommodate the workers and their families. These workers and their wives and families came from the length and breadth of Great Britain as well as from a variety of Lancashire districts.

They included specialist tradesmen, fitters, coach builders, engine fitters, wheelwrights, blacksmiths and clerks.

By 1939 most of the houses were empty and only the Railway Signal Company was left. This was closed in the early 1960s.

The former industrial area has now been re-developed as a nature reserve with a pond, wild flowers and pathways.

CHAPTER TWENTY ONE

There's Gold in them there Hulls

The sinking of the vessel, SS *Laurentic* in January 1917 off the Irish coast was seemingly just another addition to the list of allied ships which were sunk by the Germans during the 1914 - 1918 conflict.

It also helped to underline how much the war would eventually cost not only in human costs, but also in financial terms.   What made this vessel distinctly different was its cargo. In addition to the passengers and crew, the ship was carrying about 3,211 bars of gold bullion.

In late 1916, the British Treasury was preparing to send tens of millions in gold across the Atlantic in payment for the American supplies and equipment needed by the British war effort. The United States had not at that point declared war on Germany, but American as well as Canadian factories were working twenty-four hours a day to make munitions for Great Britain and her Allies, and those munitions had to be paid for.   So in January 1917, the gold was sent from H.M. Treasury in London by rail to the docks at Liverpool, where it was loaded into the second class baggage room of the former White Star ship, the *Laurentic*.

On a typically cold winters day in January 1917, the SS Laurentic steamed out of Liverpool, bound for Halifax in Canada.

The ship made a short but fateful stop at the small port of Buncrana in Lough Swilly, before recommencing her journey across the Atlantic.

As the ship rounded Malin Head, off the coast of Donegal, it hit two floating German mines. The ship had only just sailed a short distance from the Irish coast, when a violent blast, followed by a second one was heard.

The 14,892 ton ship went down in forty five minutes and only 121 of the 475 aboard survived.

The ship had run into a minefield laid only a few days previously by the German Submarine U-80, and the second explosion had destroyed the engine room area. The power supply was destroyed, all of the ship's lights had been put out, and the engines had been made useless.

The *Laurentic* was doomed, and the situation was not made any easier by the fact that it was still dark and extremely cold, and so the officers had to swing the lifeboats out in pitch darkness.

Perhaps the ship's pumps might of have saved the vessel, but as all engineering personnel had been killed and the engine room was being rapidly filled with sea water, they could not be used. The *Laurentic*'s commanding officer, Captain Reginald A. Norton, together with the ship's chief steward, Mr. Charles Porter, descended down into the vessel's lower compartments, which were rapidly filling up with water one by one They managed to close two watertight doors and see to it that no man, still alive, was left on the sinking liner.

After doing this they got up on deck and entered the last lifeboat. The lifeboats had left the ship safely, with all the men who were still alive inside them.

Several of them had been badly affected by the cold water, and as the lifeboats were picked up the following day, many were found dead in the boats. The rough seas and extreme cold took its toll and many of the dead in the lifeboats were found to be frozen solid.

Then the *Laurentic* made her final plunge, and sank in 125 feet of water. Accounts of the event vary as to the true loss of life, however of the 722 men aboard it is said that almost half were either drowned or died of bitter exposure to the January weather.

But with such a colossal amount of government gold bullion lost, it was not long before the wreck was located and an extraordinary salvage attempt began. In the same month as her loss, Royal Naval Lieutenant, Commander G.C.C. Damant was summoned to an urgent meeting with the Admiralty and was given the unenviable task of recovering the lost gold. Little did Lieutenant Damant realise when he arrived at the admiralty offices in London, that he was about to begin a seven year salvage epic to recover the gold.

He was selected as a man with a reputation as an experienced and efficient naval diver, and somebody who had already carried out a string of successful and dangerous operations.

However, the hope was that the cargo could be better salvaged in the summertime, because of the shallow waters.

The work started of as soon as it could and by September 1917, Commander Damant and his team of divers, working in twenty three fathoms below the surface of the Atlantic, had recovered £800,000 worth of gold from the wreck. Eventually, after seven years of salvaging, 3,186 gold bars were recovered.

To this day, the quantity of gold that was recovered from the wreck stands as the greatest amount ever recovered from a sunken shipwreck.   Damant's salvage operation is well documented, and the story of the recovery appears in almost every treasure book ever published.

Today the *Laurentic* rests in a depth of 120ft of water and makes for an excellent dive for all levels of diver As the total number of gold bars was 3,211, and no more could be found, the work was considered finished. In 1932, a private group of salvagers managed to pick up another five bars from the wreck.   The remaining twenty bars still await recovery.

As is very often the case, there is more than one bizarre event associated with this story.

SS *Laurentic* was launched in 1908, and entered service between Liverpool and Montreal on 29 April 1909. She only ever served on the Liverpool-Canada route, and eventually was to gain notoriety in the capture of the infamous murderer Doctor Crippen, in which Chief Inspector Walter Dew of the London Metropolitan Police used the *Laurentic*'s speed to arrive in Canada before the fleeing suspect on the SS *Montrose*.

Hawley Harvey Crippen was an American, born in

Michigan in 1862, and qualified as a doctor in 1885, he then worked for a patent medicine company in the USA.

Dr Crippen

He had first come to England in 1900 and lived in London at 39 Hilltop Crescent, Holloway with his second wife Cora Turner, who was better known by her stage name of Belle Elmore.

Early in 1910 Belle disappeared, and Dr Crippen moved his mistress Ethel le Neve into the house, and she soon began to appear wearing his wife's clothing and jewellery.

One of Belle Elmore's friends reported her suspicions to the police.

Dr Crippen meanwhile, had been telling people that she had moved back to the USA, to nurse a sick relative.

Mrs Crippen

Detective Chief Inspector Walter Dew visited Crippen, and left the premises after Crippen had claimed that his wife had eloped with a lover, and a search had not revealed anything of a suspicious nature.

Crippen and Ethel le Neve left the country for Antwerp, and then took a cabin on SS *Montrose* bound for Canada.

The house at Hilltop Crescent was searched again however, and the remains of a female body were found to be buried beneath the cellar. Dr Bernard Spilsbury, the famous pathologist, identified the body as that of Mrs Crippen from a piece of abdominal scar tissue, and found that there were traces of a poison called hyoscene in the body.

Crippen and Ethel le Neve had fled across the Atlantic on the SS *Montrose*, with le Neve disguised as a boy. Captain Henry George Kendall recognised the fugitives and, just before steaming out of range of the land-based transmitters, sent a wireless telegram to the British authorities: "Have strong suspicions that Crippen, the London cellar murderer, and accomplice are among saloon passengers. Moustache taken off, growing beard. Accomplice dressed as boy. Manner and build undoubtedly that of a girl." The search for Crippen was assisted by the master of the SS *Montrose*, who entered into history by the first use of the telegraph to relay his conclusions to the ship's owners and the police, that he suspected that the "boy" accompanying one of his passengers, Mr Robinson, was Ethel le Neve in disguise.

Ironically, had Crippen travelled 3rd class, he would have probably escaped Kendall's notice.

On board the *Montrose*, a wait of several days ensued because the ship was out of range of wireless communication. Dew boarded the faster White Star liner, the SS *Laurentic*, at Liverpool, arriving in Quebec, Canada ahead of Crippen, where he then contacted the Royal Canadian Mounted Police.

INSPECTOR DEW ESCORTING DR CRIPPEN FROM THE MONTROSE

As the *Montrose* entered the St. Lawrence River, Chief Inspector Walter Dew, disguised as a pilot, came aboard. Dr Crippen and Miss le Neve were arrested on board the *Montrose* on 31 July 1910. At that time Canada was a British dominion, so Dew was a Scotland Yard detective operating in territory of the British Empire. If Crippen, a U.S. citizen, had sailed to the United States, even if he had been recognised, an international warrant followed by extradition proceedings would have been required to bring him to trial.

Captain Kendall invited Crippen to meet the pilots as they came aboard, where Inspector Dew re moved his pilots cap and said, *"Good morning, Dr Crippen. Do you know me? I'm Chief Inspector Dew from Scotland Yard."* After a pause, Crippen replied, *"Thank God it's over. The suspense has been too great. I couldn't stand it any longer."*

He then held out his wrists for the handcuffs. Crippen was later returned to Liverpool, England, on board the SS *Megantic*.

Doctor Hawley Harvey Crippen and Ethel le Neve were put on trial for the killing of Mrs Crippen (Belle Elmore).

The trial was of great public interest at the time, and was avidly followed by the newspapers of the day.

Crippen Trial

Dr Crippen was subsequently convicted at the Old Bailey for the murder of his wife and was executed by hanging on the 23 November 1910 (aged 48) at Pentonville Prison, London

Ethel le Neve

Ethel le Neve however, was later acquitted.

CHAPTER TWENTY TWO

Liverpool to Manchester by Rocket

This the tale of an MP, the first passenger train from Liverpool to Manchester, and the first recorded fatality involving a train journey.

The route of the new rail link from Liverpool to Manchester was chosen after a thorough investigation of all the options available, the route of the tracks had to be taken into consideration as well as various geological obstructions and defects, and in fact the whole operation was dependent upon getting all of this correct.

There were at least two major geological obstructions to overcome between Edgehill in Liverpool, and the terminal which was to be constructed at Liverpool Road, Castlefield in Salford, one at the beginning, and another at the end of the line.

At the Liverpool end of the track, there was an enormous challenge to be met, first in the

construction of a tunnel, and then making a deep cutting through solid rock at Olive Mount in Wavetree.

After that, there came the equally difficult challenge of traversing the huge mass of bogland situated at Chat Moss, just outside Manchester. The line of the tracks was finally decided after much debate and would pass through Walton, Broadgreen, Childwall, Huyton, Prescot, Rainhill, Warrington, Leigh, Eccles and then terminate at Salford.

In trying to decide how best to get passengers and freight along the Liverpool and Manchester railway, track engineers James Walker and John Rastrick, suggested a speed trial be held at Rainhill near St Helens, Lancashire.

In October 1829 the directors of the soon to be completed Liverpool and Manchester Railway held a competition to find the most appropriate locomotive to use on their railway. The prize was £500 (say, £100,000 today).

The contest was advertised in the *Liverpool Mercury*:

The directors of the Liverpool and Manchester Railway hereby offer a premium of £500 (over and above the cost price) for a locomotive engine which shall be a decided improvement on any hitherto constructed.

The Rainhill Trials, as the competition came to be known, were to be held over a number of weeks, grandstands were erected and many sightseers came to watch the events.

Ten or so railway engine manufacturers indicated that they would bring their locomotives to the Trials, but in fact only five did so.

The Rocket was the only locomotive to complete the trials. It averaged 12 miles per hour (later achieving a top speed of

30 miles per hour) and hauled 13 tons, and subsequently was declared the winner of the £500 prize.

the Stephenson Locomotive Company was the clear winner, so consequently was given the contract to produce locomotives for the Liverpool & Manchester Railway.

Just to remind us how important the whole project of building the first passenger rail line was, we should compare the journey that William Huskisson made by horse-drawn coach from Chichester in Sussex, to attend the grand opening of the line, a distance of about 250 miles; the journey took over a week in a series of horse drawn carriages.

The Liverpool & Manchester Railway was finally opened on 15th September, 1830. The prime minister, the Duke of Wellington, and a large crowd of people attended the opening ceremony, which also included a procession of eight locomotives, including the Northumbrian, the Rocket, the North Star and the Phoenix.

William Huskisson (11 March 1770 – 15 September 1830), was a British statesman, financier, and a Member of Parliament for several constituencies, including Liverpool, but he is best known today however, as the world's first reported railway casualty, being fatally injured in a railway accident while attending the opening of the Liverpool and Manchester Railway. In fact, he was run over by George Stephenson's locomotive engine, The Rocket.

The journey of "The Rocket" would begin in the Edge Hill district of Liverpool, near to Crown Street.

As usual on these occasions, it was attended by many national and local dignitaries, the principal one being the Duke of Wellington.

Mr Huskisson chose to ride down the line on the same train as the Duke of Wellington. At Parkside, close to Newton-le-Willows in Lancashire, the train stopped to observe a cavalcade coming towards them on the adjacent line.

Several members of the Duke's party stepped onto the trackside to observe more closely.

Mr Huskisson went forward to greet the Duke, and as the MP was exiting his rail-car, the locomotive Rocket approached on the parallel track.

Mr Huskisson was unable to get out of the engine's way in time, and his left leg was crushed by it.

After the accident, the wounded Huskisson was taken by the train (driven by George Stephenson himself) to Eccles, where he died in hospital a few hours later.

With large crowds assembled along the line between Liverpool and Manchester, it was decided to continue the journey of the engine 'Northumbrian' to its destination in Manchester.

However, when the train entered the Manchester area, the passenger carriages were pelted with stones by weavers, who remembered the Duke of Wellington's involvement in the Peterloo Massacre, and his strong opposition to the proposed 1832 Reform Act, (then again, they may possibly have thought they were rival football supporters). So ended the first ever scheduled passenger train journey, an eventful one to say the least, and one which paved the way for the rapid expansion of rail transport throughout Britain, and eventually the rest of the world. The tomb and monument where the remains of William Huskisson MP are buried, is the centrepiece of St James Cemetery, which is located in the grounds of Liverpool's Anglican Cathedral.

Huskisson's Tomb

CHAPTER TWENTY THREE

Liverpool - Let's Go Back 200 years

We are about to take a virtual journey back in time where we will take a look at what was then the large coastal town of Liverpool and to a period which marked the beginning of its huge leap forward to become the second city of Queen Victoria's British Empire.

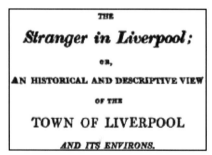

I recently discovered a book which was originally written and published in Liverpool in 1812 by the local publishers; Thos Kaye of Castle Street, and which gives the reader a fascinating account of the life and times of the city in the first decade of the nineteenth century.

It was written at the time by a visitor to the city and is a comprehensive description of the various places in Liverpool which he visited.

One of the many interesting chapters in the book concerns a visit to the docks and the waterfront and gives a good impression of how things appeared at that time to 'The Stranger in Liverpool'.

The author, Thomas Kaye, described a walking tour of the docks and waterfront which in 1812 had not yet been extended to the seven mile length of docks it later became. He began his walking tour of the city near to Paradise Street, and wrote the following description of his tour:

'Alongside many instances of civil transformation, Liverpool may be judged as one of the most eminent. The date of its existence is comparatively modern and either owing to its local advantages not having been duly appreciated, or to the general absence of the spirit of commercial enterprise it has lately emerged from obscurity; but its rise has been so unprecedented and rapid and its political and commercial relations are becoming so important, that it can no longer be passed over without observation, or observed without interest.

Here there are no valued remains of ancient, barbarous, or classic architecture; no obsolete inscriptions in characters which are half obliterated by the ruthless hand of time; nor any of the more portable relics which usually adorn notable cities, rendered sacred by the accumulated roster of ages. Its history is the history of the silent but powerful operations of industry and it stands as an monument to perseverance and enterprise.

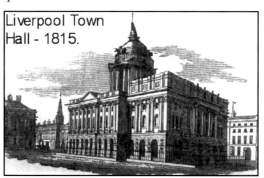
Liverpool Town Hall - 1815.

In introducing an account of Liverpool, the reader may wish to be made acquainted with the origins of its name, on this subject however, little can be advanced with certainty. The names of places, it is true, have not in general been imposed, but have taken their rise either from local peculiarities, or some occurrence on or near the spot on which they stand; but the distance of time have often rendered that uncertain.

The latter part of the name Liverpool is said to have been assumed from the circumstances of the town being situated formerly on the borders of a pool, or dock, which occupied the site of Paradise Street. There is much conjecture as to the origins of the name of the town,. in the charter of Henry II. 1173, it is said to be a place which the Lyrpul men call it Litherpul.

Now Litherpul in the dialect of that county, signifies Lowerpool, this being the name before the town was incorporated, and consequently before the liver was assumed as a part of its arms, the author concludes this to be the true derivation, and that all the modes of spelling since observed have been accidentally introduced.

But it is perhaps the best conjecture, that as the whole estuary of the Mersey, was anciently called Lyrpul, Lyrpoole, or Litherpul, the hamlet of Liverpool, being the largest collection of buildings immediately upon this pool or haven, obtained likewise the name of Lyrpul, by which it is, even to this day, known amongst the country people.

Still, however, we want the reason for the change of name, through all its varieties, from Lyrpul, Litherpul, Liverpull, Lyvrepol, Lyverpole, Leerpool, to Leverpool, and eventually Liverpool.

This could not have been wholly the effect of accident, or why has not the village of Litherland been also converted in the same manner?

Walking onward in the same direction towards the River Mersey we come to an extending building which is the tobacco warehouse in the Kings Dock, although Queen's Dock with which it is connected by one common basin, being fairly removed from the town, is more clean and less encumbered with adjoining buildings than the docks we have already passed.

These docks are chiefly for the berthing of American ships, and with which they are often crowded, and present a pleasing view of the port's growing commerce with the United States, and of the mutual advantages with which each country derives from that amicable connection, which has generally subsisted between them since the independence of America was acknowledged.

They appear to have learned from their mother country on how to unite the practical with the graceful, as their ships are generally large, well built, and finished with elegant accommodation for passengers and crew.

This part of the riverside is lined with public houses, shops and warehouses etc and is very broad and convenient for the ships to dock.

It is generally occupied by large vessels which seem to be chiefly British, and frequently they exhibit in their magnitude and construction, fine specimens of the profession of naval architecture. As well as the extensive commerce of the port to which most of them belong.

We pass on, and turning to the left through the street directly opposite the drawbridge we arrive at the Salthouse dock.

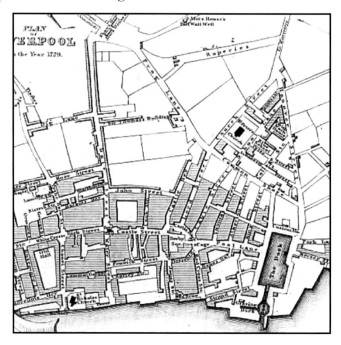

Several of the neighbouring streets present us with a spectacle of vice and misery in their lowest forms, and from which the heart turns with a disgust which almost overpowers one's feelings of commiseration with those who are participants. Great as the advantages of extensive commerce are, it is deeply to be lamented that dissipation and licentiousness should be its almost constant companions.

It certainly becomes a duty of the magistrates and of the philanthropist, to adopt those measures which may render it less glaring and less offensive.

Equally it is to be regretted that a more vigorous means of moral instruction is withheld from that valuable character the British Sailor, who too often for want of restraint, has abandoned himself to his passions and destroys the hard earned wages of a long and dangerous voyage in these vile orgies.

This vast expanse of docks exhibits all the bustle and variety which you would expect from modern mercantile transactions, and like those of the other docks, it is surrounded with warehouses and anchor makers, blacksmith shops and block and tackle makers, numerous sail makers, and of course public houses .

Continuing our tour and proceeding nearly eastward, from the south end of the Queen's-dock, we enter Parliament-street, which forms the boundary of Liverpool; that part of the town on the right being called Harrington, an estate formerly belonging to the Earl of Sefton, but now in the hands of several proprietors, who have erected buildings upon it. This is yet an unfinished street, but is wide, with a good pavement, affording a convenient carriage-road to the docks. The buildings in the neighbourhood are chiefly cottages, warehouses, and manufactories. On the left, near the middle of the street, is an extensive iron-foundry, called the Liver-foundry and as we ascend, the houses are more spacious and respectable.

The road which crosses this street near the top, leads on the left into the town, and on the right to Toxteth-park, belonging chiefly to the Earl of Sefton. In the angle stands St. James's church, in a retired and rural situation.

Taking the left-hand direction, we come to an opening where St. James's and Great George's-streets meet.

The latter, with the adjoining square, we shall have occasion to notice in the sequel : turning, therefore, down the former, which takes its name from the church we have just noticed, we have before us a long and closely-built street, which has the peculiarity of terminating with a church at each end.

The fine spire of St.Thomas's church is here seen to advantage, but the tower and the body of the church are obscured by a lofty warehouse, and other adjoining buildings. The upper part of the street is well built, and has many genteel houses; but the lower part, which has the name of Park-lane, is narrower, worse built, and less respectable. On the right, as we proceed, we observe several good streets, bearing the names of some of our most distinguished admirals. Nelson-street and St. Vincent-street lead immediately into Great George's-Square, and Cornwallis Street yet unfinished, presents a pleasing opening into Duke-street.

Through the opening of St. Vincent-street a view is obtained of St. Mark's church.

The streets on the left hand lead throughout the line to the King's, Queen's, and Salthouse-docks, and are for the most part, from their situation, narrow, dirty, and crowded with inhabitants.

Turning on the right, through Dickenson-street, we cross Frederick-street, and enter into Pitt-street, an extensive and populous street where, a little lower down, we meet with a spacious and elegant chapel, belonging to the Methodists, called Pitt-street Chapel.

Following the same direction, we enter into Cleveland-square.

This square, which is 100 yards by 40, forming an area of 400 square yards, was formerly a place of genteel residence.

In the centre was a rusticated obelisk, and a row of trees was planted in front of the houses.

Opulence has now found more eligible situations; the obelisk is removed, the trees are nearly destroyed, the houses are mostly converted into shops, and the square is now a market for provisions.

From Cleveland-square we pass through Price's-street, to the head of the Old Dock at Paradise St where, as it is nearly in the centre of the town, and at an almost equal distance from its principal streets, we shall at present leave the stranger to continue his business.

This fascinating book is based on a stranger's account of Liverpool, written in 1812, just before the Battle of Waterloo (No, not chucking out time at The Liver Hotel in Crosby, the other one.)

The book became the property of a Mr SA Green, a gentleman living in Boston, Mass and he donated the book to the library of Harvard University in Cambridge Massachusetts in 1887.

Bringing our waterfront journey up to date, and to the twenty-first century, let us take a look at the current downtown Liverpool Waterfront.

Within the last ten years the city centre of Liverpool has undergone a massive programme of transformation. In fact the main building project involved undertaking the largest construction operation in Europe.

The new complex is now 'up and running' as they say,

and is known as *Liverpool One*.   To me, it resembles a huge multi-storey temple, where great hordes of people come every day to carry out the rituals of mass consumerism, and to worship at the altars of whatever God of Fashion is currently deemed to be omnipotent.

CHAPTER TWENTY FOUR

The Capital of Ireland

 The Wellington Rooms, or as it is often commonly referred to, The Irish Centre, was situated on Mount Pleasant, Merseyside, close to Liverpool Metropolitan Cathedral. The building was designed by the architect Edmund Aikin, and built between 1815–1816 as a subscription assembly room for the Wellington Club. It was originally used by high society for dance balls and parties. Neo-classical in style the building's façade is Grade II listed, but the building is now derelict, a poor reflection on the changing wealth, and cultural values of the city.

During the 1840s, Irish migrants began arriving in the city, by the tens of thousands, due to the Great Famine of 1845-1849. Almost 300,000 arrived in the year 1847 alone, and by 1851 approximately 25% of the city was Irish-born. The Irish influence is reflected in the unique place Liverpool occupies in UK and Irish political history, being the only place outside of Ireland to elect a member of parliament from the Irish Parliamentary Party to the British Parliament in Westminster. A Mr T. P. O'Connor represented the constituency area around Scotland Road, from 1885 to 1929.

Ireland's rural population had rapidly grown in the nineteenth century, with potatoes being the staple diet of the rural population.

However, this crop was very vulnerable to disease, and no cure existed in Ireland for the dreaded 'potato blight'. Even if a cure had existed, the people on the land would not have been able to afford it. In 1844, a new form of potato blight was identified in America and it basically turned the potato into a mushy mess that was almost completely inedible, and useless to all intents and purposes as a staple food.

The people of Ireland expected a good potato crop in 1845. However, when it came to digging up the potatoes, all they got was a black gooey mess. The crop of 1846 was all but a total failure, and yet again there was a very poor harvest in 1847. Three disastrous years in succession presented Ireland with huge food problems. The government in London initially decided to do nothing. The logic behind such a decision was that Ireland had suffered from potato famines before, and would have the necessary knowledge on how best to get by in this case. However, by 1846 it was plain that this was no 'ordinary' famine.

The Prime Minister, Sir Robert Peel, believed that if corn was released onto the Irish market in stages, it would keep down the price of other foods. This actually worked reasonably well but it also showed the lack of knowledge that existed in London with regards to Ireland.

While Peel was at least doing something to try and help, he also had little knowledge of the country he was trying to help. The corn was welcomed as better than nothing. However, there were very few mills of any sort in Ireland, so simply grinding it down into flour was very difficult.   Many people in Ireland became seriously ill attempting to eat the corn without it having first been ground down. The government also tried to help by establishing public work schemes and road building projects in an effort to create employment, so that some families got some money. However, two issues hampered any work done by the government:

1) The general view in Westminster of the Irish, was simply that they were <u>not worth the effort</u>, and that anything that happened there was their fault.

2) The government was very much driven by the doctrine of Free Trade. There were those who argued that if the Irish could not survive on the way they lived, then they should fall by the wayside. Free Trade meant in effect,the survival of the fittest - a practical example of Darwinism.

Those who produced these vital products simply got a better price for them in England than in Ireland. Driven on by free trade, foodstuffs continued to leave Ireland - despite the fact that it was desperately needed in Ireland itself. Also during the time of the famine, £1 million of corn and barley were exported from Ireland to mainland Britain, along with quantities of dairy produce. The whole issue was not helped by the majority of English landlords in Ireland who showed no real sympathy for those who worked their land. Those who could not pay their rent were evicted. Some landlords resorted to the forced emigration of their tenants, in an effort to 'solve' the problem of Ireland. In the October of 1847, one such ship, *Lord Ashburton*, sailed from Liverpool, carrying 477 Irish emigrants to North America, with 177 of these people coming from one estate, (which not surprisingly, was owned by an absentee landlord).

Some of them were so poor that they were all but naked for the journey, and eighty-seven of them had to be clothed by charity groups in America before they could leave the ship. The *Quebec Gazette* described the vessel and all that it represented as *"a disgrace to the British Authorities."* The absentee landlord, by the way, who had forced 177 of his tenants onto the ship was none other than Lord Palmerston, the British Foreign Secretary at the time, and one of the most famous of Britain's politicians in the nineteenth century.

Many had fled Irish estates out of fear of imprisonment, then begged all the way to Dublin or other seaports on the east coast of Ireland. Once there, they boarded steamers and crossed the Irish Sea to Liverpool, Glasgow, and South Wales. It was a short trip, just ten or twelve hours long and cost only a few shillings, although pauper families sometimes travelled for free as human ballast on empty coal ships, while others were given fare money by landlords, hoping to get rid of them cheaply.

In one case, a crowded steamer heading for Liverpool arrived at the dock with 72 dead aboard. The captain had ordered the hatches to be battened down during a storm at sea, and they had all suffocated below deck.

Despite the dangers, the Irish knew that once they landed on Britain's shores they would not starve to death. Unlike Ireland, food handouts were freely available throughout the country. The quality of the food was also superior to the meagre rations handed out in Ireland's soup kitchens and workhouses.

The Irish first headed for Liverpool, a city with a pre-famine population of about 250,000, many of whom were unskilled labourers.

During the first wave of famine emigration, from January to June of 1847, an estimated 300,000 destitute Irish arrived in Liverpool.

Sadly, many of the poorest of the poor in fact never made it to North America. Overnight, sections of the city featuring cheap lodging houses had rapidly become jammed with overflowing crowds who had moved into musty cellars, condemned and abandoned buildings, or in fact anywhere they could just lie down.

Amid these densely packed and unsanitary conditions, typhus once again reared its ugly head and an epidemic followed, accompanied by an outbreak of dysentery. The cheap lodging houses around the Waterloo Dock area were used by the scores of Irish emigrants waiting to embark on ships heading for North America. Three out of four Irish sailing for North America departed from the seaport at Liverpool, where often they had to sleep over for at least a night or two, until their ship was ready to sail.

Many of these emigrants contracted typhus in the rundown, lice-infested lodging houses, then boarded ships, only to spend weeks afterwards suffering from burning fever out at sea.

On June 21, 1847, the British government, intending to aid besieged Liverpool, passed a tough new law allowing local authorities to deport homeless Irish people back to Ireland.

In Liverpool, the poverty of the emigrants was visible in their bodies, in their rags, and malnutrition, in their toothlessness, matted hair, body smells, and other clearly visible signs which clearly set them apart.

Glasgow, the second major port of entry into Britain, also resorted to deporting the Irish, due to similar overcrowding and fever outbreaks.

Everyone feared fever, and shunned the Irish no matter how much they pleaded for help. Working men also viewed them as rivals for unskilled jobs. So in order to avoid deportation, the Irish moved further into the interior of England, Scotland and Wales, but invariably, wherever they went they were not welcome. A large but unknown number, arrived in Liverpool to cross the Atlantic with their tickets or their fares only, but were completely unprepared for even slight setbacks.

The routine delays in sailing dates were especially dangerous and accounted for the many thousands caught in between official and criminal coercion, and from which few emerged unscathed, and a considerable number literally penniless.

Many were also vulnerable to the devious practices of the freelance crooks who infested the lower levels of the emigrant trade, and being unused to complicated transactions, as they were to schedules or lodging houses.

These poor souls very often fell foul of money changers, offering to change their English coin into American currency of less or even no value, or of lodging-house keepers who might keep a family 'on tick' for food and shelter, and strip them bare when payment came due, by force if necessary, if threats failed.

Many of the petty frauds practised on them were despicable, their baggage would be stolen by the runners (thieves)and then "commissions" demanded for its return; half-fare children's tickets were sold to illiterate adults who would then be turned away at the gang plank. Worthless out-of-date tickets were casually altered and bought by the gullible or desperate. Others were refused passage because they lacked the additional one dollar "head money" required at American ports.

In their rush to fill the ships, brokers were known to book emigrants for New York onto vessels bound for Baltimore or Boston, or even New Orleans, assuring them that these places were only hours apart.

The fleecing of "greenhorns" was widely practised in all the big cities in both Europe and America, sometimes as in Liverpool by their own people who had probably survived a similar experience themselves not long before. It soon became a kind of initiation rite for simple migrant peasants into the niceties of city life.

Liverpool's well-earned fame for this skullduggery could probably not have been achieved but for the overabundance of fresh and easy victims. Medical or ship's officers could reject one or all in a family without appeal, often just moments before they boarded.

Health officers could order immediate quarantine into the city's fever sheds, or to the ship hulks, moored in the river, to isolate the infected.

Doctors, or beadles, could remove "lunatics" from the poorhouses and even from the dockside, and take them to the crowded asylum at Rainhill, where the wards were filled with hundreds of poor souls who were diagnosed as suffering from "mental paralysis".

Orders for their removal back to Ireland were issued by the hundreds, and within days, the first boatloads of paupers were being returned to Dublin and Cork, then abandoned on the dockside.

In that year, in excess of 15,000 poverty stricken Irish people were dragged out of filthy cellars and lodging houses on Liverpool's waterfront, and sent back to Ireland, even if they were ill with fever.

With a million people dying of starvation, and one million emigrating to North America, the Irish population declined by two million during the famine period. This affected Ireland, as those who were most active and who could contribute the most to Ireland, tended to be those who left the country. The political impact of the famine in Ireland was considerable, and was to last for many years. Finance for a number of Irish republican movements in the late nineteenth and twentieth centuries, came from the east coast of America, primarily Boston and New York, who believed that the only people who could help the Irish were the Irish themselves. Not surprisingly, many of the leaders of the Easter Rebellion of 1916 had ancestors who had been deeply affected by the Great Famine before they emigrated to America.

One of the many macabre stories which arose from researching Irish historical links with Liverpool, is the mysterious mass grave which contained over three thousand six hundred coffins, which accidentally discovered during a site excavation for a new building at St Oswald Street in the Old Swan district. Strangely, there were no known maps or parish records available showing this particular burial site.

The site had never been a known graveyard, and no one could determine just why thousands of people had been buried there. Stranger still, all the bodies were neatly grouped according to their ages, which ranged from children of ten or twelve to adults in their twenties and thirties. The coffins were all unmarked, and stacked sixteen feet deep.

The grim discovery was made in October 1973, while clearing space for a Catholic primary school. The demolition men were ordered to leave the site immediately and a cordon of secrecy was thrown around the area.

Archaeologists in London read of the astounding mass grave in Liverpool, and immediately journeyed to the city to investigate.

When the archaeologists from London arrived in Liverpool, they were horrified to learn that the thousands of corpses had been exhumed and cremated.

The ashes were later reburied in a special container at Anfield Cemetery. The authorities did all of this under a cloak of secrecy but the Home Office refused to comment until the 1990s, and then admitted that the entire set of files relating to the case had been lost. This much, is known for sure about the St Oswald Street events of 1973, and importantly, that it can also be substantiated by documented evidence. Later, of course, many theories circulated in Liverpool and beyond about the circumstances surrounding these deaths and the burial of those many thousands of poor souls. There are usually two basic reactions to this type of event involving either the creation of an 'urban myth', or the more sinister 'conspiracy theory'. The conspiracy theory however is not necessarily the same as the urban myth as the urban myth is a fantasy created by the written word or word of mouth only. The conspiracy theory usually involves factual events, but then creates a set of alternative causes, mostly malign. In this case, they range from the mass execution of Irish immigrants around the year of 1847, by British soldiers by order of the government, to them being the victims of some secret satanic ritual.

The truth is that in the City of Liverpool in 1847; there were 5,239 deaths due to typhus, and 2,236 deaths caused by diarrhoea or dysentery. Overall, something like 100,000 people in the city contracted typhus, diarrhoea, dysentery or measles. The worst affected areas were the Vauxhall, Scotland and Exchange districts of Liverpool. It is almost certain that the mass graves found in Old Swan would have been filled with the victims of this terrible and tragic event.

Over a period of time the situation gradually improved for Irish people and their descendants, and eventually they became almost totally assimilated, and consequently, more acceptable to the majority of the British population.

Today, in the 21st century, those British people whose ancestors made the short sea journey from Ireland to Britain, are now almost indistinguishable from the rest of the population, a dubious achievement some might think.

Thankfully, almost all the barriers which existed for their grandparents and great grandparents, have gradually dissolved over time.

In the 21st century, the only tangible and lawful barrier for those of Irish descent (or English descent for that matter) who have remained as Catholics is their religion, which, by The Act of Settlement of 1701, means that a member of the monarchy who

wishes to marry a Catholic will forfeit their place in the line of succession to the throne, and also in practice, from becoming the Prime Minister of Great Britain (should they ever wish to have either of those doubtful privileges).

Ah well, I suppose you can't have everything.

CHAPTER TWENTY FIVE

When I was a Lad, We Never Had...

I am amazed at how many things have changed since I was a lad, things which we take for granted today, both positive and negative. The majority of consumer items I have listed below were introduced into our society after the end of World War Two, and particularly during the late sixties and early seventies. The ones which come to my mind first would be: Cars, computers, calculators, microwaves, fridges, holidays abroad, national health service, eating meals out, credit cards, frozen food, home telephone, mobile telephones, iPods, DVDs, electronic calculators, dish washing machines, clothes washing machines, central heating, betting shops, alley gates. Stealing from people's houses was almost unknown as there was little or nothing to steal.

Blackberries, other than for putting into fruit pies, ambulance chasers (doubtful claims from insurance companies), television, holidays abroad - nor at home if it came to that, welfare benefits, single mothers, eating out at restaurants and cafes, fast food restaurants, chocolate, no fruit, other than local apples once a year.

In Britain almost all foods were rationed except bread and potatoes (but even bread was rationed after the war), most clothing (including shoes and boots), furniture and coal.

All iron railings were removed by the government, to be

made into various weapons and war materials. Millions of tons of metal - a legacy of the Victorian era's love of wrought iron - and all aluminium pots and pans were collected to be melted down and made into aircraft engines and components. Old woollen clothing was unpicked by volunteer knitting circles and then were re-knitted into warm woollen gloves and socks for the troops.   Sheets were patched and then finally turned into bandages. Envelopes were reused and newspapers were collected (by small children) and taken to the Town Hall.   Where possible any scrap food was collected and taken out to farms for feeding the pigs.

Mind you, we did have: Ration books, pig-swill bins in the street, an annual charabanc trip to Blackpool, The Dandy, The Beano, The Knockout, Film Fun, fades (manqué old fruit outside the fruit shop), the Blitz, corporal and capital punishment, pumps (not trainers), street parties, Saturday morning pictures at the cinema, military national service, horse and cart deliveries, barrage balloons, cod liver oil and orange juice, ragmen with horse and cart, football boots with steel toe caps, chip butties, coal fires in the grate, a bath once a week (whether you needed it or not), concrete air raid shelters in the street, conductors on buses and trams, gas masks for everyone, including children, identity cards, snoek - a strange breed of fish - which even the cat would not eat, tram cars, the overhead railway, boys in short trousers till the age of 12, women in head scarves, whistling paperboys, children's May processions, cocky-watchmen, Pasha Turkish cigarettes, home made toffee apples, hanging for convicted murderers, clothes   rationing, the blackout, (no lighting showing from the house), no street lighting, food rationing, German bombing raids at night, carbuncles and boils on the back of your neck, and not so much 'stars in their eyes'- we were more likely to have 'styes in their eyes'.

Well, that is the last spoonful of this particular bowl of scouse, I hope that you found it a fairly enjoyable experience.

I certainly enjoyed gathering together the ingredients, and then preparing it for you. If you have bought this book, (the net profits are donated to a Liverpool based charity) then you have made a contribution to helping children in the developing world, and also to homeless people in Liverpool.

Can I say thanks on their behalf.

Index